The Beatles Are Here!

50 Years after the Band Arrived in America, Writers, Musicians, and Other Fans Remember

—Edited by—

PENELOPE ROWLANDS

ALGONQUIN BOOKS OF CHAPEL HILL   2014

Published by

ALGONQUIN BOOKS OF CHAPEL HILL

Post Office Box 2225

Chapel Hill, North Carolina 27515-2225

a division of

WORKMAN PUBLISHING

225 Varick Street

New York, New York 10014

Library of Congress Cataloging-in-Publication Data

Rowlands, Penelope.

   The Beatles are here! : 50 years after the band arrived in
   America, writers, musicians, and other fans remember /
   edited by Penelope Rowlands.

     pages cm

   ISBN 978-1-61620-350-4

   1. Beatles—Influence.   2. Rock music fans—United States.

   I. Title.

   ML421.B4R68 2014

   782.42166092'2—dc23   2013033601

10 9 8 7 6 5 4 3 2 1

First Edition

For Julian, always,
& for my sisters in screaming:
Vickie
Joann
Linda

"All those beautiful songs that helped me exist . . ."
—CYNDI LAUPER

CONTENTS

· ·

INTRODUCTION

. . . .

WE WERE THERE.

We were there when the Beatles first landed on American shores, half a century ago.

This book is about the impact of their arrival. It is a "scrapbook of madness," in John Lennon's famous words.*

Our madness, and theirs.

People who weren't around then can scarcely imagine how it was when the Beatles came. How quickly they changed . . . everything.

Suddenly, they were here. There. Everywhere. The band infiltrated the airwaves by way of AM radio, at first via just a few songs, including, notably, "She Loves You," with its famous "Yeah, yeah, yeah" chorus and insistent, captivating beat. Two minutes and nineteen seconds that seemed to render almost everything, musically, that came before it obsolete.

It erased so much.

---

* When asked in a 1971 *Rolling Stone* interview where he and Yoko Ono would like to be when they were sixty-four, Lennon said, "I hope we're a nice old couple living off the coast of Ireland, or something like that, looking at our scrapbook of madness."

The world was so different then—as so many witnesses to the Beatles phenomenon attest in the following pages. The Atlantic seemed impossibly vast. There was no Internet, of course. News traveled by way of long-distance calls (rare because of the expense) and telegrams. Telegrams!

Beginning in late 1963 the songs arrived, ultrafast, delivered to us via quick-talking DJs and in vinyl form—45s, EPs, LPs. Each album came in mono or stereo. Whatever the format, each Beatles song was a burst of fresh sound, with a danceable beat, sweet, easy lyrics. I can still recall how electrified—shocked!—I felt by the first one I ever heard; from its thrilling opening drum roll to its curious last chord, "She Loves You" took me somewhere else.

One release followed another in staccato succession—"I Want to Hold Your Hand," "Love Me Do," "I Feel Fine," "Eight Days a Week"—a sustained climax that went on and on. Which partly explains the intensity of the experience. Within a quick slice of time the band changed the way we dressed, moved, listened, thought. The way we were.

One writer in these pages, Sigrid Nunez, likens the experience of Beatlemania to drinking a potion. It was that transformative and abrupt. Joe Queenan describes a revolution: "The Beatles swept away Pat Boone, Vic Damone, the Kingston Trio, doo-wop, and all that other twaddle in about thirty-six hours."

We carried around the Beatles' songs on plastic transistor radios with their scratchy sound. We moved to the music. We came alive to it on boardwalks "down the shore" in New

Jersey, in sleepy Southern towns, on farms in Oregon, in Detroit cityscapes. We blared it out to our American world from streamlined, finned, gas-guzzling cars; suburban houses with pristine lawns; urban apartments overlooking sooty alleys. And some of us heard it in our heads as we chased the Beatles down hotel corridors or yelled up to them from the sidewalks below.

We were so primed to scream. As quite a few people in this collection, including "Cousin Brucie" Morrow, the legendary disc jockey, and the musician Billy Joel, remind us, the band's arrival in February of 1964 seemed to awaken this country from a profound, shattering grief. President Kennedy had been assassinated only six weeks before. America was in shards.

I remember coming home from school through the streets of Manhattan on the day JFK was killed, walking among hollow-eyed, tear-stricken adults. Grown-ups who had apparently emerged from a black-and-white horror film, lurching along, as if barely alive themselves.

Within a few short months, I was running through those same New York streets with a pack of girls I scarcely knew, following the Beatles and other British rock and roll bands around town, shrieking at the top of our lungs.

Which is how *The Beatles Are Here!* came about. Many years after the photograph on the cover of this book was published in the *New York Times*, I wrote about both that image and my Beatlemaniac years for *Vogue*. Several years later, the girls in the picture (actually, all but one) found one another again. We had stood side by side almost fifty years earlier on a sunny city street, fellow Beatlemaniacs, united in screaming. When we met again, through miraculous, Internet-era kismet, we felt a bond.

One that endures to this day.

Our story, among so many others, threads through this collection. It is our scrapbook of madness, comprised of written essays, interviews (the two can be distinguished in the pages that follow by the icons before each one: a microphone for interviews, a pen for written texts), and other fragments—including an email, a Facebook exchange, a handwritten diary entry. Some of the voices here are famous, others are not, but all touch on how profoundly affected we were by the arrival of the Beatles in our midst. And by "we," I don't mean just those who experienced them firsthand: a few of these contributors weren't even born when the band tore into town. Yet they, too, experienced them vividly, if at some remove.

One person after another bears witness to a cultural event so enormous that it's hard to imagine an equivalent. The writer Verlyn Klinkenborg exults—counterintuitively, at the very least—over *not* attending a performance of the band he revered when they played near his California town. For Véronique Vienne, a Frenchwoman who came to live in New York City just when the Beatles arrived, the group provided a soundtrack to a strange and surreal-seeming way of life.

Singer Cyndi Lauper, standing distractedly by a highway near Kennedy Airport, missed seeing the band's limousine as it roared by. No matter. Ringo, John, Paul, and George were omnipresent in her bedroom in a nearby Queens neighborhood in the fan photos she'd taped, adoringly, to the walls. It's tempting to believe that, even in two-dimensional form, they asserted their power, awakening this future superstar to love and music.

They did the same for so many of us.

For me, as this book's editor, culling this material was a quiet education, instructive in countless ways. It was fascinating to see how often disparate narratives aligned with each other, then diverged. And I was intrigued to learn from a host of musicians why the Beatles' music was so powerful then— and remains so to this day.

The singer and songwriter Janis Ian explains precisely how that chord works, the one that sends chills down our spines at the beginning of *A Hard Day's Night*. The glorious soprano Renée Fleming, who has recorded her own stunning, dusky rendition of the Lennon-McCartney ballad "In My Life," marvels at the perspicacity of the Beatles' lyrics, as does the omni-talented young composer and songwriter Gabriel Kahane. And musician Tom Rush takes us poignantly back to the moment when folk music was the unlikely center of popular radio culture. It was doomed, of course. It was soon to be engulfed by you-know-who and the clamorous rockers that came after.

These narratives hold a mirror up to our society as it was back then. The reflection in some ways came as a shock. How could I have lost sight of how jaggedly divided the country was in this period? The Civil Rights Act hadn't yet been passed.

De facto segregation was the order of the day, a full decade after the Supreme Court, in *Brown v. Board of Education*, put an end—on paper, at least—to racial segregation in American schools.

Numerous commentators recall the fraught racial atmosphere of the early 1960s. Yet for the novelist Judy Juanita, who grew up in East Oakland, California, and edited a Black Panther newspaper in college, the Beatles provided hope. To her, their music, with its roots in American R&B, provided gorgeous, unexpected proof that black music and culture, willfully ignored by the white media for so long, could be kept down no longer.

The U.S. population itself was so different! Gay men and women were near invisible, at least to many. Female professionals were scarce. The Roman Catholic population, never quite in the mainstream, had been energized by the 1963 election of John F. Kennedy, one of their own, to the White House. So many ethnic groups that are now such a vibrant part of American life—Latinos, Middle Easterners, Indians and others from the subcontinent—hadn't yet arrived in significant numbers.

One strong evocation of the era is provided by Gay Talese, these days a gray eminence, a man of letters, but then a fledgling journalist for the *New York Times*. Recalling the experience of reporting on the Beatles for that paper, Talese re-creates the New York they found on their arrival, with its riots over the draft and civil rights, its burgeoning working class, and its very own (these days, almost paltry seeming) one percent.

Talese's Beatles story, which accompanied that photo of us

screaming girls, is reproduced in these pages. It yields some surprises. For one thing its language is remarkably fresh, as if it had been written just yesterday, and it's replete with the wry observations and witty turns of phrase that would make Talese—along with other writers such as Nora Ephron and Tom Wolfe who, as young newspaper reporters, also covered the Beatles' arrival in New York—famous as a practitioner of what came to be known as the New Journalism.

A glance at some of the other articles in the same issue of the *Times* demonstrates how radical Talese's approach was for the period. On a smaller, yet telling, note, it's disconcerting to see how many errors the piece contains, probably ones inserted in the course of editing the piece or setting it in type. ("Hot type," as it was then.) Yet these glitches, too, have a point to make, emphasizing the exercise in time travel that is at the heart of *The Beatles Are Here!* For each typo reminds us that not so long ago—and well after four young men from Britain came along to upend our lives—we had no spell checks, or indeed computers, at all.

I listen to the band's songs as I write these words, wondering why they mattered so much then—and do to this day. I focus on their first songs because these are the ones to which I, and so many, first awakened. Today, on the far side of the Beatles phenomenon, I'm struck by the purity of their early musical offerings, the seductive simplicity of the stories they tell.

In "Something," there's a woman who moves. Little else intrudes beyond the emotion that that movement, and person, inspires. In "Till There Was You," there are birds, singing, and a female who makes the singer (Paul) hear them as if for the first time. The Lennon-McCartney songbook of the period is full of those who want to hold us tight, be our man, whisper words of love. And they want to do so "Eight Days a Week"!

These lyrics are unabashedly romantic. Yet the Beatles themselves, even then, were somewhat different, as we would later learn. "They weren't innocent at all," remarks Anne Brown, one of a core group of die-hard Beatlemaniacs interviewed for this volume. As she wryly points out, "They did *not* want to hold your hand."

Oh, well. At least at first, they pretended they did. Later their music darkened, became jagged, gothic by comparison. And psychedelia, which the Beatles would soon take up—or is it the other way around?—seemed to lead straight to the apocalypse. It deconstructed the mind, each individual, all the world, and it presaged the violence to come.

But most of the music that acts as a subliminal soundtrack to *The Beatles Are Here!*—the songs evoked over and over by writers and fans in these pages—was written before rock music darken and metallic, out of control . . .

In 1964, when the Beatles first landed on our shores, America was reeling, in mourning, divided against itself. Some of us, growing up, felt we needed to run—away from our homes and families, toward something new. No wonder the band meant as much to us as it did! We needed its simple, hand-holding message. We needed its love.

And there it is, in the Beatles' gentle early songs: "Please Please Me," "All My Loving," you name it. Each is a distinct universe, shiny and pristine, each one a haven. You can walk right in, and be safe.

Which I think partly explains why these musicians mattered so much then—and still dominate half a century on. Their music seduced us all those years ago. It won us over. Then it changed just as radically as its audience did, moving through violence, protest, drugs, spiritual awakening, and more. It brought us to the next phase, long before some of us even suspected that change was in the air.

It's amazing, yet entirely right, that this band is still on top. *The Beatles Are Here!* indeed. In many ways, they never left. Today, they're as vivid, appealing, and powerful as the very first song of theirs that some of us ever heard:

"She Loves You."

We loved them.

We were there.

The Beatles Are Here!

Tools of Satan, Liverpool Division
by Joe Queenan

. . . .

MY FATHER WOULD not let me and my three sisters watch the Beatles when they appeared on *The Ed Sullivan Show* in February 1964. His official reason for imposing this interdiction was because the Catholic Church had identified the Beatles as tools of Satan. This was strange because even at that very early juncture, the Beatles, with the possible exception of John, seemed quite harmless and even cuddly. I cannot recall in what capacity, or through what specific channel, the Church had singled out the Beatles as minions of Lucifer; their proscription may very well have obtained only at the Tri-State level, with reports of their villainy appearing in a popular Philadelphia publication, the *Catholic Standard & Times,* which kept tabs on satanic activity in the Delaware Valley.

Whatever his reasoning, my father, a devout though not especially satisfactory Catholic, told us in advance that he would be commandeering our tiny black-and-white television on each of the three consecutive Sunday nights in question, preventing us from participating in one of the most famous events in the history of the medium, if not the planet. He was devout, he was doctrinaire, and he was breathtakingly mean.

My older sister says that I circumvented this edict by sneaking over to our uncle Jerry's house and watching the Beatles on his television set on that first Sunday evening. I seem to recall that my three sisters, fourteen, nine, and six at the time, got left out in the cold, an injustice that may have scarred them for life. They have no clear memory of seeing that first show. But I have never actually raised the question with them. My uncle was no more a fan of pop music than my father—he was the only Republican in our family and positively worshipped the duplicitous, vindictive Richard Nixon—but he was not an out-and-out jerk. He recognized that these broadcasts were important to us, and he treated them with commensurate gravity. He understood that things are serious to those who take them seriously, even if they seem frivolous or ridiculous to you personally.

Moreover, as a hotshot salesman for Philadelphia Gas & Electric, he knew a hot product when he saw one. He could see what was coming—a tidal wave—and he understood that it was time to get out of the way. The Fifties were over, the age of the silver-throated crooner had passed, and the Big Bands were not coming back. I seem to recall my uncle snickering at the Beatles' silly hair and cutie-pie laminated suits during their legendary *Ed Sullivan* appearances. But in no other way did he interfere with our viewing pleasure.

Today I remember no specifics about the other two broadcasts, other than that I enjoyed every second of them. My mother may have arranged it so that my father was not at home those second two Sunday evenings. But I do recall that the thought of not seeing those programs was inconceivable at the time. I was thirteen years old when the Beatles came to the United States and to this day I believe that my life as a sentient human being, and not merely as my parents' chattel, began at that moment. This would not have happened had Herman's Hermits or the Dave Clark Five been the first to arrive on these shores. Whatever the Beatles had, no one else in my lifetime had it, with the single notable exception of Michael Jackson, who possessed a similar ability to mesmerize an entire planet. (Born in 1950, I was too young to remember Elvis's first big splash.)

To my best knowledge, only Jackson, Presley, and the boyish Frank Sinatra ever exerted this kind of hypnotic sway over an entire society. Madonna, though ubiquitous, was never beloved. And no one ever lined up to see her movies. My daughter went through her childhood desperately waiting for her generation's equivalent of the Beatles to show up. They never showed up. The Backstreet Boys and 'N Sync showed up instead. The closest she ever got to the Beatles was Jimmy Eat World. And the Vines. And Matchbox Twenty. And so on.

The arrival of the Beatles was the first time I felt that the world might belong to me. Until I heard "She Loves You" on my sister's transistor radio in December 1963, I had no interest in music, period. Until that moment I viewed music as an annoyance at best, and at worst as a punitive child-rearing device. I had grown up in a house dominated by Frank Sinatra, Tony Bennett, Patti Page, Perry Como, and Mel Tormé, along with more explicitly sinister figures such as Doris Day, Jerry Vale, and Vic Damone. On Saturday nights, as part of his sadistic pop cultural brainwashing program, my father would force us to gather in the living room and watch *The Lawrence Welk Show*. Welk, an uberschmaltzy accordionist and bandleader from Strasburg, North Dakota, with a pronounced German accent, was as corny as the day was long, performing treacly versions of wunnerful, wunnerful, wunnerful standards with his Champagne Music Makers, milking them to the very depths of their ghastly insipidity. To this day, rebroadcasts of the shows are among the most popular programs on public television, suggesting that the dream of public television has not yet been fulfilled.

My sisters and I grew up despising Welk and all those of his ilk, so when the Beatles showed up, we felt the way the French must have felt when the GIs swarmed into Paris in August 1944. The Beatles liberated young people from Victor Borge, Robert Goulet, Steve and Eydie, and the demented sing-along-with-the-bouncing-dots schlock immortalized by Mitch Miller. The Beatles liberated young people from bland show tunes, ethnic hooey like "Volare" and "Danke Schoen," and stultifying novelty tunes like "Hello Muddah, Hello Fadduh" and "Mr. Custer."

The Beatles held out hope that life might actually be worth living, that popular culture need not be gray, predictable, sappy, lethal. To this day, what I feel toward the Beatles is not so much affection or reverence. It is gratitude.

People like my father hated the Beatles because they had long hair and silly suits and came from a foreign country and were young. But mostly they hated them for the same reason the hair bands of the 1980s hated Nirvana: Because they could see the handwriting on the wall. They could see that the Beatles were a cultural writ of execution for a society that idolized songs like "How Much Is That Doggy in the Window?" and "Blame It on the Bossa Nova."

The Beatles swept away Pat Boone, the Kingston Trio, doo-wop, and all that other twaddle in about thirty-six hours. Or, let's say, they marginalized it. To this day, my English wife, who saw the Beatles in concert at age thirteen, cannot listen to Frank Sinatra and Dean Martin and Andy Williams, or to songs like "The Girl from Ipanema," without wincing, because in her view, the whole point of the Beatles was to bury that stuff forever.

Some adults understood this. My mother once told me that she knew that the world no longer belonged to her when Elvis first appeared on the scene. People of my age have the same feeling about hip-hop; the world stopped belonging to us when our kids started listening to N.W.A. But for my father Elvis was merely the first shot across the bow. Elvis and Chuck Berry and Motown and Bob Dylan, all predating the Beatles, were no more than flesh wounds; the Beatles were an arrow right through the heart. At some level he must have understood that the world would never be the same after the Beatles, that while Sammy Davis Jr. and Lawrence Welk might live on in some vestigial capacity, they would no longer rule the roost.

He dreaded the Fab Four; they were emissaries of doom. Yet, for some inexplicable reason, he did not mind us watching the Rolling Stones when they appeared on shows like *Shindig!* and *The Hollywood Palace* and *Ed Sullivan.* This may have been because by the time the Stones and the Animals and the Kinks showed up, the Beatles had already taken Normandy. The Stones and the Animals and the Kinks were like the Greeks who came streaming through the streets of Troy after the warriors concealed inside the Trojan Horse had thrown open the city gates. The bands that followed the Beatles were darker and raunchier and scarier than John, Paul, George and Ringo, who were really quite wholesome. Be that as it may, it was the Beatles who lay concealed inside the Trojan Horse, not the Stones, the Kinks or the Animals. It was the Beatles who burnt the topless towers of Ilium.

With the Beatles, the group's second album, but the first truly great one, was released in the UK on November 22, 1963, the day John F. Kennedy was murdered. My father, the son of Irish-Catholic immigrants who arrived in a nation that despised them, never recovered from JFK's assassination. He took Kennedy's murder personally, sensing perhaps that Kennedy would be the last Irish-Catholic president he would see in his lifetime. When I was older, I was struck by the irony in this, because I have always believed that the Beatles' stupendous success in America was directly related to JFK's death. I remember reading this theory years and years after the fact and thinking, "Yes. Here is one theory about pop culture that is not stupid or obvious."

The Beatles helped heal America. Or at least young America. Or at least most of young America, because there were still plenty of people in Dixie who were more than happy to see JFK go. Healing is what music does best. It stops the bleeding. The Beatles did not stop the bleeding all by themselves; the Supremes, the Miracles, the Temptations and the Four Tops pitched in too. But the Beatles got the process started. Some musicians heal ethnic groups. Some musicians heal nations. The Beatles healed an entire planet.

People love to romanticize the 1960s, but the only part of it you could actually enjoy was the music. Everything else was hell. Lynchings. Assassinations. Vietnam. George Wallace. Nixon. Jersey Boys. At least that is my take on it.

The first song I ever paid the slightest bit of attention to was "She Loves You." I heard it right around Christmastime in 1963. I was thirteen years old. It was the first time in my life I heard a song that seemed to speak directly to me and not to adults. To this day, as much as I love "Honky-Tonk Woman" and "Purple Haze" and "White Rabbit," I still think that "She Loves You" is the greatest song ever written. For me, it is and always will be the song that changed the world. I love that song. I absolutely love it. And with a love like that, you know you should be glad.

Greil Marcus, rock critic

. . . .

ONE THING I will never forget about being a student [at the University of California, Berkeley] was reading in the *San Francisco Chronicle* that this British rock 'n' roll group was going to be on *The Ed Sullivan Show.* And I thought that sounded funny: I didn't know they had rock 'n' roll in England. So I went down to the commons room of my dorm to watch it and I figured there'd be an argument over what to watch. But instead there were 200 people there, and everybody had turned up to see *The Ed Sullivan Show.* "Where did all these people come from?" I didn't know people cared about rock 'n' roll. I thought it was quite odd. . . .

. . . I go back to my dorm room and all you're hearing is the Beatles, either on record or coming out of the radio. I sit down with this guy who's older than me—he's a senior, I'm a sophomore—and he was this very pompous kind of guy, but I'll never forget his words. It was late at night and he said, "Could be that just as our generation was brought together by Elvis Presley, it may be that we will be brought together again by the Beatles." What a bizarre thing to say! But of course he was right. Later that week I went down to Palo Alto—I had grown up there and in Menlo Park, on the Peninsula—and there was this one outpost of bohemianism, a coffeehouse called Saint Michael's Alley, where they only played folk music. But that night they were only playing *Meet the Beatles*. And it just sounded like the spookiest stuff I'd ever heard. Particularly "Don't Bother Me," the George Harrison song. So the spring of '64 was all Beatles. But the fall [when the Free Speech Movement erupted on the Berkeley campus] was something else.

We Saw Them Standing There
by Amanda Vaill

. . . .

IN FEBRUARY OF 1964 I was a boarding student at Madeira, a girls' school on the Potomac River, west of Washington, D.C. A bookish, rather nerdy adolescent from New York City, I'd grown up the only child of two increasingly estranged parents. As a minority of one I necessarily absorbed my parents' tastes because, at home at least, there was little to set against them. I knew virtually nothing about popular music, or the culture that spawned it. I would rather listen to Ravel than the Ronettes; and while I wished like anything that I could have been on a barge in the Thames to hear the original performance of Handel's "Water Music" back in the eighteenth century, I had absolutely no experience of (and professed to have less interest in) the dating rituals described in Lesley Gore's hit single "Judy's Turn to Cry." When my classmates listened in rapture to Frankie Valli and Bobby Vinton, I gritted my teeth; I hated these teen heartthrobs' amped-up accompaniments and melismatic vocalizing.

Back in November, though, thumbing through a copy of *Time* magazine during study hall instead of doing my Latin declensions, I'd read about a group of young rockers from Liverpool who were convulsing Great Britain, and had just played for the Queen Mother and Princess Margaret at the Royal Variety Performance, where their lead singer, John Lennon, had had the audacity to crack a joke: "For our last number," he'd said, with a Liverpudlian burr, "I'd like to ask your help. The people in the cheaper seats clap your hands. And the rest of you, if you'd just rattle your jewelry." I thought that was pretty cheeky and pretty classy at the same time. And in their photographs, this group, who called themselves the Beatles, looked both those things, with their modishly mod close-fitting jackets, their dark skinny ties and sharp white shirts, their mops of long but well-groomed, squeaky-clean hair (no Vitalis-slicked pompadours for them). It didn't hurt that they were English, too—I was the worst sort of snotty Anglophile, able to name all the English kings from William the Conqueror on, but wobbly on the American presidents.

As Beatlemania had become an entrenched phenomenon and a signifier of hipness, some of my more enterprising schoolmates had managed to acquire copies of the first Beatles single to appear in the United States; and when we came back from Christmas vacation the dormitory hallways throbbed with the sound of Ringo Starr's drums and John Lennon, Paul McCartney, and George Harrison protesting that they wanted to hold our hand. The sound was nothing like any of the American rock 'n' roll I had heard, despite the electric guitars and the 4/4 beat. The harmonies were bright and fresh, the drum track as filigreed as a Bach fugue, and the sound was direct, unfussy, unengineered. I, who had had no use for Elvis or the Kingsmen or the Crystals, became infatuated.

Maybe it had something to do with the fact that most of their songs seemed so forthrightly joyful, and we all—certainly my schoolmates and I—needed a little joy just then. It had been only a little more than two months since we'd been stunned by the news, on a bright autumn Friday, of John F. Kennedy's assassination in Dallas. The whole nation was in shock, but the blow hit particularly hard at Madeira, where so many girls were the daughters of congressmen, senators, and diplomats. We'd heard about it in midafternoon, and in the early evening a few of us gathered in the Wing Library, a gracious paneled room whose windows overlooked the twilit river, to talk and comfort one another. At one point we became aware of the quiet snarl of an airplane in the distance, the sound growing louder as it passed overhead, then diminishing as it flew over the river to Maryland. All air traffic around the capital had been shut down in the uncertainty following the assassination, so there was only one plane it could be: Air Force One, carrying two presidents, one alive and one dead, back to Washington. Suddenly no one wanted to talk any more.

Just over two months later, on Sunday, February 9th, clad in the pastel shirtwaist dresses and Pappagallo flats we wore for dinner and for Sunday vespers, we crowded into that same room, where a small television set was tuned to *The Ed Sullivan Show*. Sullivan, a former gossip columnist with brilliantined hair and the mournful eyes of a funeral director, had become a household word—had even inspired a song in the Broadway musical *Bye-Bye Birdie*—by retooling the vaudeville variety-show format into a conduit that delivered the performing arts into more than fifty million living rooms across America. Every Sunday night at 8 p.m., from coast to coast, in a bonding ritual that helped to define popular culture in mid-century, Americans shared the experience of watching the opera divas, circus acrobats, Shakespearian actors, magicians, ballet dancers, pop singers, and standup comics that Sullivan deemed worthy of headlining his show. And tonight, in addition to a number by the zaftig British comedienne Tessie O'Shea and an excerpt from Lionel Bart's musical *Oliver!*, Sullivan was introducing the Beatles, who had flown across the Atlantic for the purpose, to America.

When the broadcast studio's pale damask curtains parted to reveal the "youngsters from Liverpool," standing on a stark set composed of cutout arrows, Sullivan's audience began to screech like a pack of gulls wheeling over a clam roll. "One, two, three, four!" came the count-in, and then the Beatles launched into the jaunty "All My Loving." They shook their glossy hair—uncannily like that of the English moppets who had just performed "I'd Do Anything" from *Oliver!*—and the studio audience shrieked again. My pastel-clad peers and I looked at the screen as the TV cameras panned over the auditorium, normally full of people who looked like our parents, and what we saw was ourselves reflected back at us: teenaged girls and young women, dressed in proper little wool jumpers or tidy tailored suits with circle pins on the collar, all gasping and clutching their faces in paroxysms of innocent desire, primal but somehow not prurient.

The Beatles went on to perform "Till There Was You," with

a sweet, straight-up solo by Paul McCartney (naturally I had to be the one to point out that the Beatles hadn't actually written that song—it was from the 1959 Tony-winning Broadway show *The Music Man*); then rocked into "She Loves You." And that was the point when we all (me included) were truly transformed, singing along, shaking our hair, just like our sisters on the screen, as if we were caught up in something bigger than ourselves, a kind of movement, and this music was our anthem.

Sullivan's show ended at nine o'clock, which happened to be when the bell sounded signaling it was time for us to return to our dormitories. This was not done by some rude electronic klaxon: instead a uniformed personage known as the Bell Maid, who normally sat behind the school's 1930s switchboard, came out from her post, crossed the corridor, and tugged on a rope connected to a bell in the cupola high above. She was ringing her peal as we emerged from Wing Library. We certainly didn't think of it then, but in some ways, she was ringing a funeral knell for one era, our parents', and ushering in a new one, which for better or worse belonged to us.

A Newspaper Article
by Gay Talese

The New York Times (by Jack Manning)

BEATLES IN DEMAND: Fans gathered outside Paramount Theater yesterday afternoon

THE NEW YORK TIMES SEPTEMBER 21, 1964

BEATLES AND FANS MEET SOCIAL SET
Chic and Shriek Mingle at Paramount Benefit Show
By GAY TALESE

Coolly elegant women in mink coats and pearls, together with men in black tie and in no need of a haircut, found themselves in the Paramount Theater last night sitting amid 3,600 hysterical teen-agers, who should perhaps have been home in bed or doing their homework.

But the Beatles were at the Paramount, the show was for charity and all was tolerated.

It took 240 policemen to keep things tolerable, however, as teen-age girls, even five hours before the 8:30 P.M. show began, lined Seventh Avenue and West 43d and 44th Streets, causing traffic jams and confusion in the Times Square area.

They screamed and squealed [sic] at everything, these hundreds and hundreds of girls between 13 and 18, some wearing "Ringo, for President" buttons or carrying banners that read, "Beatles Please Stay Here 4-Ever."

Pandemonium Grows

At 8:30 P.M., when the theater darkened, the girls inside shrieked and cheered. When a shaft of light flashed onto the bandstand they shrieked and cheered even louder. When the announcer just mentioned the word "Beatles"—even though they were not to be on until 10:45 P.M.—the whole house reverberated with the thumping, jumping, flailing, shrieking crowd of young people.

Anyone beyond 21 years of age yesterday felt ready for Social Security.

Those included, in addition to the policemen and the Beatles' chauffeur, many of the adults who put on the $75,000 benefit for Retarded Infants Service, Inc., and United Cerebral Palsy of New York.

It was an incongruous sight last night, one that brought together the chic and shriek sets. The latter sat mostly in seats ranging from $5 to $25 each; the former sat mostly in seats costing $50 each (380 were sold) or $100 each (224 were sold).

The Beatles, when they finally got on stage, shortly after 10 P.M, sang for 25 minutes strumming out tunes that nobody could hear. They sang 10 numbers, but as they did, teenagers rose to their feet and jumped and twisted in the aisles; others tossed jelly beans, slices of bread or rolls of toilet tissue toward the stage.

Flashbulbs illuminated the theater, from the orchestra up to the remote reaches of the upper balcony, and policemen stood elbow to elbow in front of the high stage, neither frowning nor smiling, just looking tired.

For everybody, the Beatles, and their adoring fans—it was a long hard day and night.

Fooled by Chauffeur

The Beatles, who had been in Dallan [sic] and stopped over in the Ozarks earlier yesterday, landed in a remote cargo area to avoid the mobs at Kennedy Airport. Then, at 5:30 P.M., they left by helicopter for Manhattan.

At that time, there were 4,000 teen-agers squashed behind police barricades along 43d Street and Seventh Avenue near the theater.

Unwisely, they assumed that these spots would give them a view of the Beatles' entrance. But at 6:10, the Beatles' chauffeur, Louis Savarese (whose biggest thrill behind a wheel came when he drove the King of Burundi to the World's Fair this summer), slyly slipped the rented Cadillac through West. 44th Street, sliding up on the sidewalk just beyond Sardi's.

Then, as a few dozen teenagers spotted the British mopheads, and came rushing and howling toward the car, 40 policemen ringed the singers. The best the girls could do was smear fingerprints over the car, and rock it back and forth a bit. By then, however, the Beatles were safely indoors,

Many girls—there were relatively few boys at the Paramount last night—were in obvious pain at having missed the Beatles' entrance: a few of them began to weep. Others just howled louder than before.

Awarded a Scroll

By 8 P.M., the theater was filled. The pre-Beatle show included songs by Steve Lawrence and Edie Gorme, Leslie

Uggams and the Tokens, Bobby Goldsboro, the Shangri-Las, the Brothers Four, Jackie De Shannon and Nancy Ames. All of them worked without fees, as did the Beatles.

Following their performance, the Beatles were honored with a presentation of a scroll by Leonard H. Goldenson, chairman of the United Cerebral Palsy Associations. It read:

"To Jack Lennon, George Harrison, Paul McCartney, Ringo Starr who, as the Beatles, have brought an excitement to the entertainment capitals of the world and who, as individuals, have given of their time and talent to bring help and hope to the handicapped children of America."

After their 10th number, the Beatles ran off the stage and left the building at 10:45 P.M., before the crowd inside could get to them.

The chic set was not interested in chasing them, for they—those who had either $50 or $100 tickets—had a champagne party in the downstairs lobby to attend.

In seven limousines, the Beatles and 14 members of their entourage sped to the Riviera Idlewild Hotel, for a night of rest before flying back to England today.

Only two people were in the lobby when the Beatles arrived, neither of them Beatmaniacs. They were reading newspaeprs [sic] and went back to them when the Beatles disappeared up the elevator.

In Love with Gorgeous George
by Penelope Rowlands

· ·

(the girl in the middle in the photo)

THE ARTICLE, WRITTEN by Gay Talese, ran in the September 21, 1964, issue of the *New York Times*. Headed "Beatles and Fans Meet Social Set," it described how almost four thousand "hysterical teenagers, who should perhaps have been home in bed or doing their homework," had gathered at the Paramount Theatre the night before. Arriving hours before the group was due on stage, they "screamed and squealed at everything."

A photograph shows a row of young women doing exactly that behind a banner reading "Beatles Please Stay Here 4-Ever." The girls have an operatic look: They might be a row of divas, mouths open wide in song, arms flung dramatically wide.

I'm standing dead center, pushing forward, with a frenzied expression. I'm flatchested, freckle-faced, and curly haired— a very young thirteen. For months I've been screaming and squealing every chance I get. I've snuck into hotels with groups of similarly obsessed girls. I've chased after autographs, any possible souvenir, including a square of fabric from John Lennon's boxer shorts that I bought for a dollar from an ad in a fan magazine. The thought that this might be a hoax crossed my mind, but only briefly. I knew for a fact that this cloth had once touched a Beatle's flesh. Somehow, I could tell.

When I first opened the *Times* and saw this photo, after school in my family's crowded apartment on Manhattan's Upper East Side, it could have been a thrill. But it distinctly wasn't. I prayed that my mother would miss it, but she was no sooner home from her secretarial job at St. James's, the Episcopal church our family had attended for five generations, than the phone rang with family friends passing on the news. By the time my new stepfather—I couldn't bring myself to pronounce his name—returned to our apartment for the first time, I was on my way to being grounded for eternity.

It was the first day of their, our, new conjugal life. They'd headed off on their honeymoon the week before, leaving us three children in the care of our maternal grandmother. Racing off to Bucks County with a man we scarcely knew, my mother called out: "Be sure you don't go down to the Beatles' hotel while I'm gone!"

I ignored her, of course. I couldn't have done otherwise, for George Harrison was the most important person in my life. While I first fell for his looks—he was twenty, jocular, glossy haired—my devotion went far below the surface. I knew that he would understand me as no one else did, and that I would do the same for him.

Loving George was more than just a feeling, it came with a future, a life. I'd imagine us making the scene together in Swinging London—the locus of everything that mattered back then. I kept his picture in a cheap gold frame from Lamston's and kissed it every night.

So I really had to go.

I headed down to Delmonico's, the hotel where the band was staying. I'd spent time down there a month earlier, too, when the Beatles were last in town. For two days that August, the corner of 59th Street and Park Avenue became an encampment. Thousands of girls clustered behind barricades. Police patrolled on horseback. Tourists stopped by.

It became de rigueur to at least have gone over to look. At one point both of my brothers went down to see if they could find me in the crowd. (They couldn't.) I was astonished that my studious older brother, Eliot—an opera fan, to my intense mortification—had made the pilgrimage. Nine-year old Richard became an instant convert. "It was exciting!" he recalled, years after the fact.

The next month, when I went down there again, I took the IRT instead of the safe, familiar Fifth Avenue bus. Riding the subway made the adventure even more illicit—I wasn't meant to take it alone. Still, with my mother and that man safely away in Pennsylvania, I felt free to do as I liked.

I stepped off the train at the Bloomingdale's station, climbed the filthy, trash-strewn stairway to the street, then headed a block west. I could almost feel the frenzy of a thousand restive girls as I turned the corner onto Park. The crowd, when I reached it, seemed monstrous, alive. Thrilling! Policemen patrolled in pairs; passersby stopped to stare.

I took my place among the pack, my sisters in screaming, girls who, in memory, look remarkably alike, with the straight hair I envied; their Beatles-inspired bangs cascaded glossily down past their eyebrows. When I arrived they were talking excitedly among themselves. John—someone was sure of it— had been sighted on the eighth floor. We stared up, as one, and waited. Whenever we saw a shadow move, or a curtain ripple, we'd shriek.

We'd been screaming together, all over New York, for the past six months. Just weeks earlier, we'd waited in a quiet frenzy at Forest Hills Tennis Stadium, where the brightly lit stage looked silvery in the humid, late summer night. When the Beatles walked out, four tiny stick figures in the distance, we rose as one. We heard only a chord or two of music. Mainly there was this enormous roar, and we were part of it. After forty minutes or so the figures retreated, the stage went dark, and we emerged from our collective trance. I would be hoarse for days.

Why did we scream? In my case, it seems clear. My world was closing in. My American mother had brought us back to her native New York from England, yanking us out of her un- happy marriage, some years earlier. Lately she'd become unrec- ognizable, sipping bourbon with her new husband—a "Mad Man" before the term was coined—each night in a ritual they call "The Cocktail Hour" and laughing at things that don't seem funny at all. I slink past them, hoping not to be noticed, yet craving attention in a way that feels almost physically like pain. I head for my room, a shrine to the Fab Four, its walls covered with pictures from fan magazines (including my favorite, which offers an "A to Z on Gorgeous George"). Enveloped by the Beatles, in love with George, I am safe.

In my free time I roam the city in quest of one band or another. One Sunday, my best friend, Addison, and I, lurking outside the Ed Sullivan Theatre on Broadway in hopes of encountering the Dave Clark Five, find ourselves, anticlimactically, face-to-face with an elderly French singer instead. We ask for his autograph but, in truth, we couldn't care less.

Standing around us are girls wearing tweed caps over their long black bangs. With their dark eyeliner and kabukiesque foundation makeup, they've got The Look, the one that I, in spite of my white lipstick and mod touches, can never quite pull off.

They don't look our way as we chat with this creaky Frenchman whom no one has come to greet. None of us, clearly, is worth a glance. The singer signs his name twice, once each for Addison and me, and when he's done he fixes me with a long stare. "You're beautiful," he says, with a twinkle in his eye that I later learn is legendary. "You're not like them," he adds, still twinkling, inclining his head toward the cluster of girls. "You're a flower." And then he is gone.

His opinion counts for nothing, but I'm buoyed up just the same. "I can't believe Maurice Chevalier told you you were beautiful," Addison repeats the whole way home on the Madison Avenue bus. But the best is yet to come. A day or so later, sneaking around in the city after school, I miraculously come across the lead singer of Gerry & The Pacemakers as he and his entourage walk briskly down the hallway of a Midtown hotel.

"Are you getting married?" I ask, falling in step beside him, in response to a rumor that's flashed among us girls.

"If you'll have me," he teases, then steps into an elevator and is gone.

I soar. Gerry is from Liverpool—our Mecca—and his "Ferry Across the Mersey" is played every other minute on our favorite radio stations, WMCA and WABC. Joke or not, his proposal is valuable currency at school, where my life is deteriorating daily. I daydream through classes; my report card is a series of Cs and worse. When I'm told that I'll have to repeat a grade the following year, it doesn't matter to me at all.

By the next summer, when the Beatles return, everything has changed. My mother has returned to Earth, and my stepfather, while never quite beloved, has at least been integrated into our lives. And I'm newly sophisticated. With my faux Courrèges dress, ivory tights, and matching white lipstick, I at last have The Look.

On a stifling night in August I head out, yet again, to hear the Beatles play. A friend and I take our places in the volatile crowd, this time at Shea Stadium. The ant-size figures emerge. They play "Can't Buy Me Love," but all we hear this time, too, are the opening chords. The thrill of it all lasts long after a helicopter arrives to whisk the band away.

A full year later, I'm back at Shea. It's August once more and, of course, sweltering hot (air conditioning isn't yet widely used). I remember one moment at the stadium quite distinctly, even as I've forgotten so much of the rest: the instant when, standing in the sweating, frenzied crowed, I realized that I no longer cared in the same frantic way. I shrieked, of course, but only intermittently. Suddenly, it all felt embarrassingly young.

Today, decades later, the Beatles are revered throughout the world. But they were never adored as directly and simply as they were by us, the very first wave of Beatlemaniacs, who chased them down streets and hotel corridors and drowned out every word they tried to sing. There were thousands of us— each one was unique—but the arc of our passion was the same. There was a time for us when the Beatles were everything. But then, as we had to, we moved on.

A Letter

from Vickie Brenna-Costa

. . . .

Vickie Costa
xxxxxxxxx
xxxxxxxx
October 15, 2007

Penelope Rowlands
c/o Vogue
4 Times Square
New York, NY 10036

Dear Penelope,
I more than enjoyed your article "Nostalgia" in the August Issue of Vogue.

Still sipping wine from my very late supper on Monday Oct. 8th, around 10:20 pm NY time. . . . I was leafing through Vogue when I came to your article on the Beatles.

It quickly took me back in time to those very days you spoke about . . . for I too was a bonafide Beatlemaniac. However, when I turned to page 106 and saw the photo of the "row of divas" it was so surreal . . . as I saw myself right there, Brownie camera in hand!

I screamed to my husband "I'm in Vogue magazine!". He said "C'mon, don't be ridiculous." I had to look again. No, there I was standing next to my childhood friend so I knew it was me.

I almost flipped out! You see, I never saw the original article in the Times. And here I was 43 years 17 days later! . . . My 15 minutes had arrived!

I am your "screaming sister" on the left side of you (with camera) And I remember talking with you that very day, for I too was very much in love with George.

Your Forrest Hills/Shea Stadium descriptions were right on! It was a very special time in a young girl's life. And yes—as we had to—we moved on.

For me to happen upon your article was sheer serendipity!

Thank you so much for writing this.

Sincerely,

Vickie Costa
p.s. Did you get an archival print of the photo?

Henry Grossman, photographer

· ·

I WAS A busy photographer in 1964. I looked back at my list of job numbers. In the two weeks around my Beatles takes I was photographing Kennedy at the White House, Lyndon Johnson here, a Broadway show there. . . .

Time magazine sent me to photograph *The Ed Sullivan Show.*

I knew who the Beatles were, kind of, from the news, but not a lot. I had no expectations when I went in to shoot. I had no ideas about the band. I wasn't listening to their music.

I photographed the line waiting to get into the theatre. There were lines of girls waiting and screaming. While they were playing, I was photographing the audience. I saw the impact the Beatles had. The girls were screaming and crying.

I understand that what Sullivan did was that he taped one show in New York, then broadcast it in two separate sections, so that it looked like two broadcasts. He only did one tape [from New York], but he made two shows out of it.

[The first and third of the Beatles' consecutive *Ed Sullivan Show* appearances were derived from this taping in New York; the second show was broadcast live from Miami Beach.]

I was just amazed at the panoply of photographers at *The Ed*

Sullivan Show. I'd seen it before: I had photographed Kennedy during the campaign and seen how groups of photographers chased him around; at his first press conference as president there were lines of them.

I moved around during the broadcast. I shot on the ground floor. I sat in the balcony. I moved around up there. I covered it from every angle I could. After the show there was a photo opportunity where we photographers lined up to get shots of the Beatles.

At their first press conference in New York, I remember being amused by them and liking them. They weren't smarmy or nasty or anything like that. They were just fun. They had great fun, and great intelligence.

When [the photos of the *Sullivan Show* for *Time*] came out, the British paper the *Daily Mirror* called me and asked if I would go to Atlantic City for a day with the Beatles, and then a concert, and I went. (The paper had an office in New York and I was a photographer for them.) I spent a day and a night with them there.

They were playing Monopoly and cards in a hotel. I have a picture of George lying on the floor playing Monopoly with [the singer] Jackie DeShannon. Ringo was playing poker or something with somebody.

At one point I said, "So Ringo, how do you like America?" He took me by the arm and showed me a view of a blank wall looking over a parking lot. He said, "Henry, this is all we're seeing of America." I spent a day and a night with them down there.

At the Atlantic City concert there was a lot of screaming, a lot of yelling. I don't think I was wearing cotton in my ears at the *Sullivan Show* but I certainly did at the concert because of the screaming. The Beatles later said they stopped playing together because of it.

I have a picture from Atlantic City with a cop holding his ears like this. [Lifts his hands to his ears.] It wasn't from the music, it was from the screaming.

The following year, the *Mirror* sent me to spend a week with them down in Nassau, in the Bahamas, where they were filming *Help*. I got to know them. They were fooling around a lot.

When I came back to New York, I showed the pictures to *Life* magazine before sending them off to London.

Life said "Go back!"

I lived at that time at 54th Street and Seventh Avenue. The Stage Deli was right around the corner. So I went in and spoke to Max Asnas, the owner. I said, 'I'm going back to see the Beatles, down in Nassau.' He gave me bagels, lox, and salami to take down to them, so I did. They loved it!

My favorite quote is actually a paraphrase of something Emerson once said. It goes something like "Stop talking! Who you are speaks so loudly I can hardly hear what you're saying." The Beatles didn't come across that way. They weren't trying to make an impression. Looking at all of the pictures I took of them [about seven thousand in all], there are none where they're deliberately making a posture.

I have a twenty-five-minute audiotape I did later on at George's house in England. It wasn't an interview—we were just talking about philosophy and Indian philosophy and life and all this kind of thing.

I was three or four or five years older than he, but he was so far ahead of me in lifetimes of knowledge and philosophy. It's more than admirable, it's incredible.

Even Ringo. When I was taking his picture for the cover of *Life*'s international edition. I said, "Ringo, I wish I had the guts to wear a tie like that"—it was very psychedelic, a very bright tie.

He came over to me and felt my tie, a paisley tie from London. He said, "Well, Henry, if you did you'd still be Henry, but with a bright tie!"

I learned from this.

By the way, speaking of Ringo and the tie, those clothes they were wearing, the suits and the capes and all of that kind of stuff? They weren't for show, they were totally to their taste. It was what they wore at home and among friends.

Another time, I was at Ringo's house in London. I had just bought some JBL speakers in New York, some hi fi speakers, and I loved them, but I was blown away by the sound of Ringo's speakers. I said, "The sound is gorgeous, Ringo, what brand are they?"

He said, "I don't know, Henry, I just like the sound."

Which is why you buy speakers! You don't buy the speakers because you're told they're good. You buy the speakers because you like the sound!

The values they were living by were terrific. That's why I kept going back. I had so much to learn from them.

I was spending a lot of time with them. George asked me when I got to London if I could take some pictures of him and Patti [Boyd]. And I said, "Sure," so I went to visit him at his house and we took some pictures. Then he said, "Let's go over to see John." So we went over to John's house. I photographed John at home, playing with his son Julian, who was a toddler.

John and George had their guitars and they both started playing music together when their wives were in the other room and Julian was around.

After the article ran I got a call from Brian Epstein, the Beatles' manager, who had heard that the pictures were being syndicated by *Life* in London. "They've never even let a *British* photographer into their homes," he exclaimed. "Please don't let them be syndicated!"

I cajoled him for about twenty minutes on the phone about why. It turns out he didn't want the public to know that two of the boys were married. He wanted the public to think they were all available.

Next day I got a telegram from him saying, "Please disregard telephone call. I've just seen the pictures, can I have a set?"

I think it was the photographer [Henri] Cartier-Bresson who talked about how an artist can see not only what a situation is but what it is becoming. My contact sheet of the Beatles captures this. In one photo after another you can see who they are, what they were thinking, what they were relating to, how they played among themselves. I love that, I love that. I saw it from the first press conference. They had humor, they had personality.

On an early visit to New York, George said something like "What's a word for this or that? I'm trying to find a word for this song I'm writing!" I said, "Well, have you looked it up in a thesaurus?" He asked what that was. So I went out to Marlboro Books on 57th Street, bought him a thesaurus and gave it to him.

Years later my sister sent me an interview in which George said something like "It was only after a friend of mine gave me a thesaurus that I was able to . . ."

That's the best thing: There was a mutuality of interest and learning. I learned from them. I was learning from "Henry with a bright tie," that kind of thinking.

I WAS HOPING to be famous one day. At first, I was going to be a famous actor, right? When I was seventeen, my aunt sent a letter after my first show. She sent me a telegram saying "May success come slowly so you'll know how to take it." (Later I was on Broadway in *Grand Hotel* for more than one thousand performances.) I was very interested in knowing how the Beatles were taking success and what it meant to them. I was curious to see how it changed them.

I would visit George whenever I was in England. On one visit, I noticed an instrument hanging on the wall that I'd never seen. He took it down and started tuning it. He said, "It's a sitar, but I can't find anyone to teach me how to play it."

I said, "George, you make a lot of money, don't you?" and he smiled. "You could afford to find the best sitar teacher in India and bring him here to spend the summer with you here."

I read in the paper months later that George had gone to India and was studying sitar with Ravi Shankar. Now, I didn't send him to India, but we gave each other possibilities. We gave each other possibilities, that's what it is. We helped each other to understand some of the possibilities of what was going on.

The next time I went to visit George he greeted me barefoot and said, "Henry, wouldn't you like to take your shoes off?" Of course—he'd been to India.

You know the other thing? So many people who came in contact with them wanted something from them. I was just delighted to be around them. I wanted to know who they were. I enjoyed it.

My father was an artist, famous for his etchings. He had met Gandhi and Einstein and done etchings of them from life. He once had an Indian chief in full regalia to pose! I had these etchings at home. I knew about being around famous people.

As an actor, I was interested in motivations, things I could use later, store away for later use on the stage.

I studied acting with Lee Strasberg. . . . I was at the Actors Studio once and there was a scene and Lee Strasberg got us to critique the scene. "Now let us suppose that I am king," he said. Everybody laughed but then, when he entered the room as king, everyone bowed. Then he said, "Now, again, let us suppose I'm king," and he entered as a doddering old man, reaching down to pick up a cigarette butt and everybody *still* bows. He said, "See, you still know I'm king. I didn't have to say 'Aha, I'm king!'"

The Beatles didn't have to say "Aha, I'm king." They didn't

have to say a word. It ties in with Emerson's quote about how who you are speaks so loudly.

I've never met a group of people as talented and personable and connected as the Beatles. And yet as strong as each of them was individually, they worked together like that [holds up four fingers of his right hand].

My adviser at college used to use the phrase *sophisticated*, in terms of having more points of reference. That really told me what the word meant. These boys were sophisticated.

I wish I'd known fifty years ago how important they were going to be. I would have shot a hell of a lot more pictures.

Good Bye, Mitzi Gaynor
by Verlyn Klinkenborg

. . . .

I WAS ELEVEN, and it was a small town in north central Iowa, not far from the small Iowa town in which my family had been living. And Mitzi Gaynor—"Hollywood's exciting Mitzi Gaynor"—you were there, on the well-worn jacket of the soundtrack of *South Pacific*. I saw the way you turned your breasts (for you were barely clothed it seemed to me) in the embrace of Rosanno Brazzi. His mouth had a peculiar shape in that photograph, open, deliberate, unnatural. I realized later that he was singing to you. When I was eleven, I didn't know he was singing. I thought he was preparing his orifice—his orifex, I think of it now—to kiss you. Just how and why and where he would kiss you with a mouth of that shape were beyond me. I was eleven and it was barely 1964, and that small Iowa town, still so new to me then, seems remote and disconnected only in retrospect. I had already been looking at you in puzzlement for years, Mitzi Gaynor, always a little surprised when I came upon my parents' *South Pacific* lying out in the open where anyone could see it. It was just about now that you lost your power over me, whatever it was. And with you went away all the childhood, all the parental music I had ever known, stacked among albums I never ever looked at again.

The world from which I (and you; all of you) witnessed the Beatles on that first *Ed Sullivan* Sunday can never be reconstructed. (I'm sure you must have realized this, Miss Gaynor, if you met the Beatles backstage when you headlined that *second Ed Sullivan* Sunday.) The show can be revisited. I saw it again recently and almost all I could see were things hidden from me at age eleven: the Beatles watching themselves being beheld—the effect of all those Hamburg and Liverpool nights—a tight band, its members endlessly aware of each other—Paul, George, and John smiling sideways upstage, to and for each other, but restraining themselves for national television. What I didn't know about the Beatles when I was eleven was endless. I knew nothing. And so I was perfectly prepared for them. That first night, Ed Sullivan might as well have said, "And now, coming to you from the thusness of Existence . . . THE BEATLES!"

And you were there too, Shirley Jones. What little I understood about musical fame came from my family's association with *The Music Man*. My dad was a high school band director, and when *The Music Man* (the movie) premiered nearby in Mason City, Iowa, on June 19, 1962 (the Beatles played the Cavern Club that night), my dad's band, wearing white shirts and black shorts, marched in a parade of massed North Iowa bands and Hollywood celebrities, including you, Shirley Jones. I have the photos to prove it. So strike me dead when Paul sang "Till There Was You" that first *Ed Sullivan* Sunday, a song that you, Shirley Jones, sang as Marian the Librarian in *The Music Man*. I mean, what the fuck. It was as though the Beatles had worked up a version of the Bonanza theme or "I've Been Working on the Railroad" just to reassure the parents of all those shrieking, cataleptic girls in the balcony. Looking back, it seems like a moment of near-horror, hearing your saccharine, epiphanic words, Shirley Jones, sung by Paul McCartney. How easily this might have been a different sort of band—a romantic, dirge-like, Leonard Cohen sort of ensemble, singing, or rather slowly breathing (thinking itself funereally sexy), "Oh please" (pause, cigarette) "say to me" (looks at shoes) "you'll let me be" (confiding to the microphone) "your man." Thank god for the drive, the energy, the high-calorie, major 7th choogling of the first number in the second half of the show that night—"I Saw Her Standing There." It put all doubts to rest.

It wasn't simple, turning this mass music, this public music into something utterly private, which is what it became for me. There was, for one thing, the lack of a personal record player. The family stereo was in the dining room, and it seemed that whenever the Beatles shouted or screamed or hit the high "hand!!" in the chorus of "I Want to Hold Your Hand," one parent or another would come through the swinging door from the kitchen. Those uncouth noises, those high notes, belonged to me the same way so many other things did at that age. They were mine by right of embarrassment. They didn't embarrass me in themselves, but hearing them in the presence of someone else did. I was never going to be part of that squealing, smelling salts crowd, sharing publicly what I felt for the Beatles. There was no need to see the Beatles live. I had only one chance to do so, and it was no chance at all. We moved to Sacramento, California, a month or so before the Beatles' final concert at Candlestick Park. I have been forever glad that I was only fourteen at the time, new to California, unable to persuade anyone—especially my Midwestern parents—that I could find my way alone to San Francisco and the concert.

Once in California, I came at last into possession of a private record player. And until much later, long after they had broken up, I always tried to listen to the Beatles by myself. I remember, early on, still in Iowa, listening to "Please Please Me" with my brother John. I remember because John, who must have been six or seven, asked me if that was a harmonica we were hearing. With the addled assurance that Peter might have felt the night the cock crew thrice, I assured him it wasn't. (It was, of course.) I also somehow managed to leave Iowa with an electric guitar, an old harlequin Supra. I learned to play it by picking out the riff to "I Feel Fine."

I can't account for all the ways those songs found the heart of me. They weren't really about anything. I never imagined that the lyrics of an early Beatles song might be a way of Cyranizing some peach-like imaginary girlfriend. (I saved the Beach Boys, so endlessly sincere, for that.) The lyrics of those early songs expressed nothing by word. All that mattered was the pulse, the changes, the emotional dynamism, the unexpected. That becomes clear watching John Lennon singing (with Paul) "I Want to Hold Your Hand" on *Ed Sullivan*. John is not yet the walrus, not by a long shot, and yet one still wonders, *"You* want to hold her *hand*?" I was eleven, and *I* wanted to hold her hand. I had no idea there was anything beyond hand-holding (witness Miss Gaynor and Mr. Brazzi) until my parents, realizing I was a sneak thief, hid an especially medicinal guide to sex, or rather the apparatuses of sex, in their bedroom bookshelf. That book had the lyrics, or perhaps the recipe, for sex, but it lacked the music of sex and the very thing the Beatles projected: emotion. Curiously, what they projected wasn't an emotion directed at someone else. It was an emotion directed back at them, and through them their astonishing music.

I wasn't allowed to buy long-playing albums, so I collected the early songs on 45s. The difference between the British and American releases caused some chronological confusion, but each new single added to what felt like a continuing crescendo of hope and expectation, followed by a momentary strangeness that soon deepened into intimacy. The walls and ceiling of my Iowa bedroom (which I shared with my brother Roger, who had placed all his bets on the Dave Clark Five) was taped over with photos of the Beatles. It sounds like the most conventional kind of idolatry, but it was just a way of getting around the fact that I couldn't listen to the Beatles twenty-four hours a day. Sometimes my parents needed the dining-room stereo to listen to the soundtrack of *Hello Dolly!* They had their own dull musical lives, it seemed.

There's always something private in the play of children, no matter how much their play is shaped by the commercial culture around them. I was a Mickey Mouse child and a Davy

Crockett child. Being a Beatles boy might just have been the next chapter, but no. What the Beatles gave me was something that bore me away from everything I had thought about myself or the world I had lived in. I was suddenly in possession of something that no one but I could ever understand. That there were millions of other Beatles fans meant nothing. Coming into the Beatles was like coming into an unknown and unexpected birthright. It was like riding an iceberg as it falls away from a calving glacier. They somehow squared the puberty I had entered, and they made music more important than whatever else puberty was supposed to be doing to me.

Two songs in particular told me that I was now in a completely different world from the one that had existed, a world to which no parent, no adult could ever track me. Those songs are "Ticket to Ride" and "Help!," released in April and July 1965. Looking back and listening to them now, I can hear *Rubber Soul* coming, an album into which I have probably gazed more deeply than any other Beatles recording. And though the Beatles feel continuous right up until this moment, something changes with "Ticket to Ride" and "Help!" That change—what is about to come—remains frozen in the changing when I hear John's voice in those songs or listen to the beautiful lag of Ringo's staggered drumming in "Ticket to Ride," so visible in the Beatles' final appearance on *The Ed Sullivan Show.* I listened to those two songs again and again and again in 1965, still in Iowa, not even knowing that California—or the rest of my life—was a possibility. All I wanted when I had finished hearing them was to hear them again. They contain, each in its own way, a feeling I can't name or describe, the languor of regret, the urgency of despair. But above all they contain the love of music.

Jamie Nicol Bowles, fan

· ·

I LIVED IN this little town of Independence, Missouri, with ten thousand people and a little record store. We listened to this radio station in Kansas City that played the Top Thirty. We were all listening to Jan and Dean. We'd go into the little record store on allowance day to buy 45s and EPs.

The radio was kind of a glimpse into another world. Independence is now a suburb of Kansas City, but back then it was a really small Southern town. It was Harry Truman's hometown. It was lovely but limited and limiting, so any vision of another world was kind of tantalizing. And my father was very strict, being an immigrant—I figured out later that it was an immigrant thing. (He grew up in Glasgow in dire poverty and came here when he was fifteen.) By the time I was growing up, he'd become the town banker, which for me only added to Independence's claustrophobic, small-town feel.

The Beatles were a fast craze. When it happened, it happened really fast. DJs like Wolfman Jack, who was then working from a pirate radio station in Mexico, began playing some cuts from the band illegally, before they'd been officially released in the U.S. They played Beatles stuff early and suddenly the group was all any kid in the neighborhood could talk about.

In the early sixties, pirate stations had really strong signals and they came from all over the place. If they could reach Missouri, then they had strong signals. These stations were all we listened to at night.

Radio had incredible power then. It was our link to the outside world. TV wasn't where we got our information about stuff, it was radio. I remember exactly what my first transistor radio looked like—it was beige plastic and it cost thirteen dollars, which was a huge amount of money then. You'd listen under the covers at night.

At least in the Midwest, hip radio stations printed out these narrow slips of colored paper that listed the top twenty each week. There'd be a pile of them on the counter of the record store and you'd use them to choose what you were going to buy that weekend.

These stores had listening booths, too. You'd go into the booth and listen before deciding what to buy. Record players, too—everyone had one in their room and they must not have cost anything.

It was such a totally different time.

The performance venues then were tiny and if a rock 'n' roll band or someone came into town, they were always on the local radio station, you could call in and talk to them. It was very personal and accessible.

When the Beatles and the Stones came to Kansas City they played the ballpark, which now would be considered a really small venue. I think the Beatles were the first to play there. Other groups, like the Doors, played in this place in Kansas

City, Kansas, that had only about three hundred seats. And all the jazz and blues musicians played in very small clubs.

The first time the Beatles came to Kansas City, I was probably thirteen. Our seats at the ballpark were in the first balcony and we had a great view. They played all the songs we all knew and we all sang along and screamed. I don't think anybody was listening.

If we wanted to hear them, why were we screaming all the time? But we were, screaming and leaping up and down. The day after the concert was just de facto that you couldn't speak because you'd been screaming so much. It was a badge of honor because it meant that you'd been there.

You defined yourself by which Beatle you liked. And you sort of knew about people depending on the Beatle they liked. My sister liked Ringo, which was really strange, and I liked Paul and we shared a room so her side of the room was Ringo and mine was Paul. We weren't allowed to put anything on the walls so we took pictures out of the fan magazines and taped them together in long strips that we hung on the molding. My sister was actually more advanced—she liked the Stones and I thought they were creepy and that Paul was cute.

I was sent to a boarding school that was run by nuns when I was only seven. It was in Kansas City—I'd return home for weekends—and all the classes were in French, including science and math. The school was all girls and there was probably much more focus on the Beatles than there would have been at a coed school. I don't think boys liked the Beatles as much.

They all started growing their hair, but they weren't out there screaming, that's for sure.

There was a huge radio tower in Kansas City that I always thought, since I was just a kid, looked like the Eiffel Tower. I'd sneak down sometimes into one of the classrooms and there it would be through the window, this big beautiful, lighted tower. I was so unhappy at the school that it seemed like a beacon of another world.

I don't know if I made the connection then but, like the radio—and the music it played, especially the Beatles—it was offering me a vision of something beyond the Midwest.

Billy Joel, musician

. . . .

THE SINGLE BIGGEST moment that I can remember of being galvanized into wanting to be a musician for life was seeing the Beatles on *The Ed Sullivan Show*. Now, I didn't have a television when I was growing up, which is funny because my father actually worked for a television company: DuMont.

I don't know if anybody ever heard of DuMont? We had a little Levitt house and the DuMont was on the rack and you pulled it out of the wall. It broke when I was about five and my mother and my father split up and nobody fixed the TV so that was the end of TV. It was this big glass thing on the wall.

I listened to classical music. I always loved it. I was enchanted by music. I would have to say that Beethoven would be my favorite classical composer. Beethoven was titanic. He lived, he breathed, he ate music. Everything was music with this guy! I understand he didn't even leave his house a lot of the times. It was like [imitates Beethoven and friends]:

Don't bother me.

But it's a nice day.

Fuck *a nice day!*

Come on out?

Can Ludwig come out?

So Beethoven was a big influence on me. Mozart. Chopin. Debussy. I mean, that's in classical music.

But the Beatles? I'm over at this guy's house. This guy I was going to say was a friend of mine. He really *wasn't* a friend of mine. I hung out with him 'cause he had a TV. I was a Machiavellian little kid, you know: *Yeah, I really like you. Let's watch TV!* So I'm over at his house and the Beatles come on TV.

Now you gotta understand this is in something like February 1964. John F. Kennedy had been assassinated in November of 1963. The country was in a funk, we had the blues. I mean, for this man to be taken away. . . . This young, vigorous, vital man who represented youth and progress and the future—he was snatched from us. And the country *really* had the blues. And who became president? Lyndon Johnson, you know, politics as usual [imitating LBJ]: *I'm speaking to you tonight with a heavy heart and big ears.* And it was like this man didn't capture *anyone's* imagination the way Kennedy did.

Now, this is also in an era when Hollywood tried to take control of rock 'n' roll. They understood that young people liked rock 'n' roll [imitates a producer]: *Hey, the young kids like the rock 'n' roll stuff, why don't we cook up a couple of rock stars right here in Hollywood, we'll find a nice-looking boy with a great big pompadour and we'll put him out there, and we'll get some snappy tunes and he'll be a big hit, a rock star.*

And, you know, you had Frankie Avalon and Fabian. Annette Funicello. And they were putting Elvis in these awful movies! [sings] "Clambake! Clambake!" Everybody who liked Elvis was like "What the hell happened to this guy?"

Also, this was during the Civil Rights Movement, and a lot of radio would not play really good rhythm and blues. There was Jackie Wilson, Otis Redding, and Wilson Pickett. James Brown. But they weren't playing this stuff on white radio. Why? [imitates a producer]: *It got the kids all sexed up, got them all to get excited, they're going to want to do this grind dance!* So they tried to pretty it up, they tried to sanitize it. They came out with Frankie Avalon, Bobby Rydell. All these boring bullshit guys.

Then all of a sudden there's this band with hair like girls'. It really wasn't, but to us the hair looked hugely long. You know, 1964. They played their own instruments and they wrote their own songs and they didn't look like Fabian. They looked like these working-class kids, like kids like we all knew. And John Lennon had this look when he was on *Ed Sullivan* like: *Fuck all of you. This is such total bullshit to me.*

And we knew. You could tell.

And I said at that moment, "That's what I want to do. I want to do that. I want to be like those guys."

Swimming to John
by Noelle Oxenhandler

· ·

IT'S STRANGE THE day you realize you're older than the Beatle you love. But as the years go by and your Beatle grows younger and younger than you, time does even stranger things to your mind.

I was twelve when I fell in love with John. Back then, childhood lasted longer than it does now, and in real life—as in so many fairy tales—twelve was a threshold year. For me John was the threshold god, the magical ferryman who arrived precisely on time to lead me from a relatively placid girlhood into the dark, throbbing heart of adolescence.

Looking back, I can see that I was always drawn to older men who came from different backgrounds than my own. In my California elementary school, I had a crush on Mr. Red, the black custodian. Whenever someone threw up in class, he arrived with such dignity carrying his broom and a bucket of sawdust that my best friend and I were both convinced we would marry him when we grew up. When I was a little older, I attended the American School of Paris for a year and fell in love with my fifth-grade teacher, Mr. Sang. He was a British man of Chinese descent, with a shock of black hair that bounced when he laughed. Once, when I missed the bus after school, he took me home on the back of his motor-scooter. There I was, holding on to Mr. Sang in his black leather jacket as we zipped through the streets of Paris. It was paradise.

After my family returned to the States, I entered a long limbo period. During this time, I might have had a mild, junior-high crush on this boy or that, but there was no one to really capture my heart, no definite Object for the quiet but inexorably gathering force of my romantic longings. Then, over the course of a single evening, that vague limbo was suddenly transformed into a state of absolute, diamond-sharp focus.

John, John, John.

It was February 9, 1964, and I was lying on a shag rug in Santa Monica, with my parents and my little brother sitting on the living-room sofa behind me. In the next moment, Ed Sullivan waved his hand, the Beatles sprang onto the stage— and I was instantly transported through the television screen into another realm. In that realm, John had been waiting for me forever.

The predominant emotion for me that night was intense *recognition*. It was as though, on some altar in primordial space and time, I'd left a request for just this man and now at last he had been given unto me, with his mop of dark hair and his wire-rimmed glasses. In the aftermath of that night, the pure shock of recognition gradually gave way to a more comfortable familiarity, and I could begin to articulate *why* John was my chosen one. I loved that he wasn't handsome in the pretty boy way of Paul, but in a quirky, ironic way that was visible in his quizzical eyebrows and his wry, slightly crooked smile. I loved the edgy tenderness of his songs. When I listened to them, I could let my heart be swept by giant tides of emotion without a twinge of feeling corny. And when John's books came out, I loved that he was not only a singer but also an author. Since I had already decided that I was a writer, this was another powerful bond between us.

There were so many. At the time, my mother—whom I'd heard people describe as "a handsome woman"—had short brown hair. She also had a somewhat long face, lively brown eyes, a strong nose, and a narrow mouth. In sum: She looked quite a bit like John Lennon. Since she had been adopted at birth, and we only knew that she was of English ancestry, it didn't take long for me to realize that my mother was actually John's older sister. This, of course, made him my uncle: an absolutely thrilling discovery. Yet somehow—through a logic that is quite mysterious to me now—this familial connection didn't diminish by one iota the romantic connection between me and John. Above all, John was my predestined lover, husband, father of my future children.

Prior to *The Ed Sullivan Show,* the most notable feature of my bedroom had been its wallpaper, with a pattern of smiling pig-tailed girls holding bunches of pink balloons. In the weeks and months that followed the show, the wallpaper gradually disappeared under giant posters of John: John in profile holding his guitar, John in a leather jacket standing in front of the brick wall of a Liverpool pub, John making the peace sign in front of the Statue of Liberty . . .

At night before I went to sleep, I would lie for quite a while, gazing up at him, studying every feature of his face, every nuance of his expression. Then I would shuffle through the ever-growing stack of Beatle cards that I kept in a drawer beside my bed. The cards came in square packs of dusty-pink bubble-gum; eventually I had hundreds of them. Each card had a Beatles photograph on one side, with some factual information about one or more of them on the other. Before falling asleep, I would shuffle through the cards, memorizing the information as if studying for some wonderful exam. To this day, I could still probably give the correct answer if someone were to ask: "What is John's shirt size?" "How does he like to take his eggs and tea?" "How old was he when he went to live with his Aunt Mimi?"

I would never have spoken these answers aloud, however. Though I knew that these were very public facts, available to any girl who had the dimes to buy the gum, I'd gleaned them through a kind of pillow-talk. They were treasures that John himself had buried in my ear, as we lay in my bed on the brink of sleep—and I had to protect them. Beyond the boundaries of my bedroom, I didn't broadcast my love for John. And I told no one that he was my uncle. I kept all this secret, inward.

For me, this secretness made my connection to John more real, intimate and special. But there was also another reason that I didn't broadcast my love. A more excruciating reason. The truth is, I could never bear to be identified as belonging to *any* group to which I actually belonged. Even as a small child, I hated to be seen *as* a child: to be glimpsed in pajamas by my parents' friends, to visit homes where children ate weenies and Twinkies at kiddie tables.

I always shut doors, so grown-ups—even my own parents—couldn't overhear me playing. Once I woke in the middle of the night to see my parents' glowing faces: they were bending over me, holding a flashlight for two dinner guests to see. I was mortified. For me, the worst thing was to be caught seeming to be the thing I was. As I got older this only intensified. If I could not bear to be seen as a sleeping child, how could I bear to be seen as a lovesick teenager?

When the Beatles came to the Hollywood Bowl, I didn't go with the rest of my Girl Scout troop. I didn't agonize over the decision. When our scout leader first proposed the idea, I looked down at the ground as the other girls jumped in the air, giggling with excitement and clapping their hands. I knew in every fiber of my being that it would not be possible for me to carry the passionate intensity of my love into such a public place—much less to see it mirrored in the faces of a thousand screaming teenage girls.

On the day of the concert, I was edgy, jumpy. Although I knew that I absolutely could not be at the concert, it felt impossible to be anywhere else. At first I planned to stay in my room all day, holding a kind of solitary vigil. With a Beatles record playing in the background, I tried to concentrate on an activity that usually soothed me: drawing a portrait of John in a large sketchbook that already teemed with portraits of him in every conceivable pose, and in every available medium: pencil, ink, chalk, Magic Marker, crayon . . . Perhaps, on this day of all days, I'd ask to borrow my mother's precious Winsor & Newton watercolors?

It was quickly clear that I couldn't muster the patience or focus. My nerves were tingling and I felt like a racehorse, stuck in a pen. I tried riding my bike around the neighborhood, but it felt like a dumb thing to be doing when John was in town. Finally I decided to walk to the beach. In those days, parents weren't so fearful about letting their children roam; it wasn't unusual for me to make the mile-long trek from our house to the beach by myself—even though the trek ended in a dark, urine-scented tunnel.

As I walked through the winding streets of our neighborhood, it occurred to me that the Beatles were breathing the same Greater Los Angeles Metropolitan air as I was. The thought was dizzying. The day appeared to be an ordinary day—people were clipping their hedges, walking their dogs, washing their cars—and yet, as I looked around, it seemed as though everything was vibrating with the evening's momentous, imminent event.

When I came to the tunnel, I held my breath as I always did and tried to zoom as fast as I could over the bits of broken glass, the beach rocks and empty soda cans, without hurting my feet in their flip-flops. Back in the light of day, I rushed down through the sand, pulled off my shift and ran into the sea in my paisley bikini. Finally, I had found something equal to my restless, overpowering excitement. I hurled my body into wave after wave, until finally my fingers and toes grew white and I threw myself down into a dip of warm sand and slept as if sleeping off a spell.

After the night of the concert, several days passed before the rumor reached me: during the performance, a girl I knew from my neighborhood had made a frenzied leap into the moat that surrounds the stage at the Hollywood Bowl. Carol Partridge. I'd always thought of her as a rather shy girl—not someone who, in the most literal way, would stand out from the crowd. Once I heard the rumor, I couldn't get it out of my head. Though my official reaction was one of hilarious disbelief, I actually felt a kind of awe. And since I had known that I myself would not be able to bear the intensity of the Beatles' actual presence, I had no trouble understanding how it was that Carol had simply broken out of her skin. . . .

I could so vividly see how she, rising from her seat, had been compelled toward the circle of light where they sang. I could see her pale face transfigured, her thin body borne over the roaring heads and waving arms and into the moat. I could see her thrashing toward them like some brave wild creature— until the security guards leaped in and fished her out. Like Paul Revere's ride, Carol Partridge's swim took on a kind of mythical, archetypal status in my mind.

From junior high all the way through high school, I remained faithful to my secret love. When I came home from school each day, I'd stack every Beatles record I had on my phonograph and enter a kind of musical swoon that would carry me all the way to suppertime, often while simultaneously reading John's books. Once, when my father came to my bedroom door to rouse me, he said, "The day will come when you don't do this anymore." I looked at him as if he was crazy.

It's strange to me now that I don't remember when, or even how, my father's words came true. Was there a single day when I suddenly stopped listening to the Beatles? Or did the habit taper off gradually, so that I piled fewer and fewer records on the turntable until finally I listened to none? With almost religious devotion, I'd repeated a certain behavior day after day, year after year—yet the demise of this behavior left absolutely no trace in my mind.

What has stayed, however, is the image of Carol at the Hollywood Bowl. And here's the truly strange thing that time has done: In my memory, the scrawny wet Girl Scout swimming so frantically, yet bravely, in the moat is not Carol Partridge. It is I.

I'm sixty now, and after all these years it's as though I have finally released myself to reveal to the world what I was: a teenage girl, madly in love—like all the other millions and millions of girls—with the Beatle who, in her mind, exists only and forever for her alone.

Gay Talese, reporter

. . . .

I BECAME A staff writer at the *New York Times* when I was twenty-three, and I was there for nearly eight years when I first reported upon the Beatles in 1964. I was covering entertainment: writing about the Beatles was one of perhaps five assignments I did that week—it could be on opera, ballet, Baryshnikov, the Yankees, whatever. It was all a story.

The *Times* was one of six or seven daily newspapers in New York City in those days and was known as a reporter's paper. The *Herald Tribune* was the writer's paper—it was where you had a columnist like Jimmy Breslin or a very stylish writer like Tom Wolfe, and many others. I was something of a peculiar character at the *Times* in that I was a writer more than a reporter.

My specialty was writing about people. I wrote about baseball players, bridge builders, civil rights leaders. It didn't matter if what they were doing was criminal or celebratory, whether they were starting a riot or holding up a bank or robbing a building—it was all part of the daily news.

At the *Times* there was a sense that the newspaper's contents weren't as perishable as ordinary journalism. We were a paper of record. When you wrote for the *Times* you were writing for the first stage of history. All of us daily reporters were doing that, although we never thought of it that way. We just covered the hour by hour events.

So there I was, in New York with the greatest paper in the world and the freedom to write about whatever entered the city. This took all forms—artistic, militant, political, racial. It changed day to day. I was masquerading as a master of everything but really I was a master of nothing. But I had a good pair of eyes and a good pair of ears and I'd listen and observe. I was out every day and every night.

THE BEATLES WERE four long-haired originals making their entrance into the city of opportunity. Their arrival was a departure from ordinary journalism. The *Times*'s editors decided that this foppish group of longhairs—these Liverpool lunatics—were worthy of history. They anointed me to go out and write of the group's arrival in a seaport city in which ships and planes every day bring new people, new dreamers, new rattlers, new personalities, and new opportunists to the shores of Manhattan.

New York City was in a great transition from being a place in which the news consisted mainly of powerful, rich, and socially connected people to one where you were also writing about people in the streets. The streets became the news. This happened because of the war in Vietnam, which caused street protests against the draft, and the civil rights movement.

The Beatles were a spectacle and I was a specialist in covering spectacles, from race riots in Harlem to the shooting of

Malcolm X and the early protests against Vietnam on such campuses as Columbia University and NYU. I also spent a lot of time covering the construction of the Verrazano Bridge that connected Brooklyn and Staten Island. A lot of people didn't want the bridge built—eight thousand people had to be moved out of the Bay Ridge section of Brooklyn, and there were huge protests against it.

And I wrote about what was left of society—the philanthropic evenings, the charity balls. The sixties were a time of social change, turmoil, yet also a continuation of New York as the financial capital of the United States. A lot of luxury living was going on in Manhattan. The rich were thriving. At the same time there were protests against poverty, especially in Harlem, and the lack of civil rights in this so-called liberal city.

AFTER I GOT the Beatles assignment, I spent a whole day watching them as they moved into public recognition. I watched them from afar. I'm in the crowd, seeing them from a distance. I didn't talk to them, I just watched. That's what I specialized in. I don't really like to talk to people. I'm a watcher, a scene describer. When I'm writing I'm not a civilian, but a kind of performer—a participating, fantasizing performer. I'm like an actor who plays a role and the role I play has to do with the people I'm writing about.

I didn't talk to the Beatles, I didn't *want* to talk to them. I described the scene around them. I always find that it's more interesting if you describe a scene as if you're writing a movie or even taking pictures. Journalism should be scenic; it should tell a story, like a novel. It has to be visual, like a film or a painting. I had no idea whether the Beatles would live on beyond the big show, the big splash. I wanted to watch them emerge in this ever-changing city, this city of spectacle, which is what Manhattan is and has always been.

THE BEATLES WERE different from anything in the entertainment world, which was still in the era of the crooner. Frank Sinatra was thriving—he was very much a big story in 1964. But suddenly the Beatles were in the forefront. They were the latest arrival from switched-on London. They imported a clashing new culture. They personified the new fashion and styles, the long hair, this new kind of music.

The British were undergoing a revolt against tradition, a revolt against the Establishment. They were an old colonial power in decline. Their royalty was in decline. Most of what was British was in decline, except the underclasses, which were surging in theater, fashion, and music. They made a profound impression on the American underclass, middle class and, as my article pointed out, even the upper, elite, moneyed class— the grandfathers of today's hedge fund trillionaires.

NEW YORK IS a city of big splashes. I had a lot of experience seeing people make splashes, whether it was Mickey Mantle hitting a home run, or the New York Knickerbockers winning the championship from Los Angeles, which they did around that time. I covered astronauts, ballet, defectors from the Bolshoi and the Soviet system. I covered all that stuff.

More often than not the city gets tired of people who emerge as the latest fad. Performers and their music have their one night stand, then fade into obscurity. It's much rarer to be recognized for a long time, as was the case with Sinatra.

After I left the *Times,* in 1965, I spent a year writing for *Esquire.* One of my assignments was to write about Frank Sinatra. I went out to Los Angeles to try to see him, but he wouldn't see me because he'd gotten mad. So I wrote the whole piece [the famous story titled "Frank Sinatra Has a Cold"] without talking to him. I didn't *have* to speak with him. As I've said, I wasn't interested in talking with people anyway. When I work, I'm only into the story. I don't sing, but when I was reporting the Sinatra story, I was imagining Sinatra. And just as I didn't interview the Beatles and wrote about the scene instead, I didn't talk to Sinatra because I wrote about the scene around him. All I wanted was to look. I was an observer.

At about this time Sinatra's press agent in Beverly Hills put out a press release about a television special that Sinatra did for NBC, which said something along the lines of "This is not the music of mopheaded young men." Sinatra had been a celebrity since the post-WWII 1940s. Like the Beatles, he'd played the Paramount Theatre. In fact, the Paramount had been Sinatra territory, with his own screaming young people, known as the "bobby soxers." He had been there, done that.

Sinatra's place had been somewhat challenged earlier, by Elvis Presley; now he had these foreigners—these "mopheads!"—coming in. There was this lack of appreciation, if not outright skepticism, about their talent. It was reflected in this press release, which was condescending in tone and secure in its position that Sinatra was king and that these other people, the Beatles, were sort of temporary court jesters.

I thought of the Beatles as just a wondrous event of a day. But later, after months and months and months, I began slowly, as a civilian, to hear their music as it was repeated every day around the clock on the radio. I began to appreciate them, as I appreciated Puccini, Verdi, Sinatra, Perry Como, Bing Crosby, Elvis Presley—I was open to everything. I was eclectic in my interests, then as now.

My Four Friends
by Cyndi Lauper

. . . .

WHEN I WAS nine, I got some Barbie dolls and two albums for Christmas. One was a Supremes album called *Meet the Supremes,* and the other was *Meet the Beatles.* I was glad to meet both of them. The Supremes sounded like they were my age, like they were my friends, and I would sing with them constantly. Their songs were memorable and easy to sing along to. And I guess that was the first call-and-response I ever sang. The Beatles, however, were intriguing in a different way because I had a crush on them. And because the media introduced them to us individually, and we were encouraged to pick our favorite Beatle, I picked Paul. My sister and I would dress up like the Beatles for our family and perform with mops.

My sister, Elen, always wanted to be Paul, so I was John. Whatever my sister was doing, I wanted to be with her. My mom told me that I was born to be her friend, and I took that literally. Besides, I didn't mind being John, because he was married to someone named Cynthia. And that was really my name, not just Cindy. And I had a dream once that I was brushing my teeth with John Lennon and spitting in the same sink. (Later, I told that to Sean Lennon, but I think it scared him.)

By singing with my sister like that, and listening to John's voice, I learned harmony and the structure of songs. By the time I was eleven, I began writing with my sister. When Elen graduated from junior high school she got an electric Fender guitar and amp and I got her acoustic guitar when I was graduating from sixth grade. Our first song was called "Sitting by the Wayside." I guess if I heard my kid write that now I'd be worried, but we were living in the protest era.

Before that, I was always singing along to Barbra Streisand from my mother's record collection. I also performed for myself a lot with my mother's Broadway albums: *My Fair Lady, The King and I, South Pacific*. I was Ezio Pinza and Mary Martin. I was also Richard Harris in *Camelot*. At times when I sang I would act like my relatives, because they were always very dramatic. (They were Sicilian, after all.) But mostly I liked the way it felt to change my voice, and when I sang I could imagine the leading man right in front of me. My interior life and my play life were so real to me that I could make up anything. I guess the saddest thing about being introduced to the Supremes and the Beatles, though, was that all of a sudden there was a difference between my mother's music collection and mine.

In high school I listened to Janis Joplin, Jimi Hendrix, Joni Mitchell, Sly and the Family Stone, the Chambers Brothers, the Four Tops, and Cream. Motown was king, and, of course, Beatles, Beatles, Beatles. When I got older, they came out with *The White Album*, and I put each of their pictures on the walls of my room. That's where I'd daydream, write poems, paint, write songs, or play other people's songs on my guitar. Sometimes I'd hear my mom call out to me to clean my room and

I'd try to ignore her. Once I must have pushed her right over the edge because she finally came in and said, "I want you and all your friends (pointing to the pictures on the walls), to clean this room up *right now*." It was not easy for her.

MY MOM WAS pretty cool. When I was eleven and the Beatles were coming to New York, my mother drove my sister, her friend Diane, and me to the Belt Parkway where the Hilton Hotel is, by the airport, so we could see the Beatles drive by, and she left us there for a while. She knew we weren't going to run into traffic. So we waited. And waited. All of a sudden we saw cars coming and *it was them*. So I started screaming, and I shut my eyes, and by the time I realized I should open my eyes, I'd missed it. I was dressed all nice, too. I had dark jean clam diggers with pointy shoes and a sleeveless green blouse, and black plaid shirt with a man-tailored collar.

A Facebook Encounter

· ·

---------- February 25, 2011 ----------

 Vickie Brenna-Costa
How incredible to find you!

Dear Penelope Rowlands,
How incredible to find you!
I am the girl standing over the BE. Are you the girl
standing to my left over the AT?

Vickie

---------- February 25, 2011 ----------

 Penelope Rowlands
I'm amazed!

Hi Vickie --

I'm amazed! yes that's me
It's hilarious! great to meet you!
Let's keep talking,

Penelope

Vickie Brenna-Costa, fan

(the girl second from the left in the photo)

I WAS VERY young, only twelve or thirteen, when I first heard the Beatles. We were living in the Wakefield section of the Bronx. I don't remember reading about them but I do remember the first time I heard them on my little pink Zenith transistor radio. I didn't know what they looked like yet. I just wanted to hear more music. I *had* to own the 45 of "I Want to Hold Your Hand" with "I Saw Her Standing There" on the flip side. After I got it, I played it to death.

I used to see my best friend, Joann Pugliese, all the time because she lived in my aunt's apartment building, five blocks from where I lived; it was really my second home. It was one of those old Bronx buildings with two entrances off the vestibule. My aunt's apartment was on the first floor in the left wing and Joann lived on the third floor in the right wing. My aunt's kitchen window and Joann's kitchen window overlooked the back courtyard. If I looked out my aunt's window and Joann looked out of hers we could see each other. When the windows were open we would call out to each other.

One day Joann called out and then came down from her apartment to my auntie's. She was waving her arms and shrieking, "I've got the album! I've got the album!" It was the long-awaited *Meet the Beatles*. We were finally seeing them for the first time. We went ballistic! Well, now we REALLY loved them! I immediately had a crush on George and she on Paul. That's when we started trying to convince each other which one was cuter ...

What made them so special? Their sound had a rhythm or beat like we'd never heard before—they named themselves The Beatles, after all—and their words just spoke to us. For me, they were in step with a young girl just becoming a young woman. "I Want to Hold Your Hand"?—a very big deal back then, holding hands. And the lyrics to "I Saw Her Standing There"? "My heart went boom when I crossed that room and I held her hand in mine"? We lived those words at St. Mary's sock hops! Elvis, Dylan, and Motown were all great, but the Beatles thrilled us to the core.

When they appeared on *The Ed Sullivan Show* we had to have more pictures. We filled our little Brownie cameras with black and white film, shut the lights and took pictures of the TV. This was Joann's idea. We didn't know if it would work but it did, they turned out great. (BTW ... she's quite a photographer today.)

The Beatles were coming to Forest Hills. The problem was, How do we get there? It was an evening concert. We were young and couldn't travel the subways alone at night. We felt so isolated in the Bronx. I pleaded with my parents for days. "You have to take us! You have to take us!" Finally, they said "Okay, okay, we'll take you!" We ended up in the top row crying and screaming our heads off. We couldn't hear a word they sang. After their helicopter takeoff, we looked at each other. We hadn't heard anything. We left hoarse but ecstatic. My parents picked us up. We rode home in a daze.

Our next chance to see them was at the hotel where they stayed after the Forest Hills concert; we heard they would be staying there at the Delmonico Hotel on Park Avenue and 59th Street. Joann's cousin Linda joined us. We met at Joann's house and that's when Linda rolled out this huge sign that read BEATLES PLEASE STAY HERE 4-EVER. I remember being embarrassed by it. I thought it was childish. I was, like, what are we doing with this big sign! But she had made the sign and we took it and the number 2 train down to Manhattan. We stood in front of the hotel and every time someone opened a window we would start screaming even if only the blinds moved.

We were crazy and that's how you and I met. We both loved George. We connected over that. You said you had also gone to Forest Hills and had been high up like we were in the stands. I remember you were very energetic and you had curly blond hair. I remember very distinctly talking to you all afternoon. I really liked you and remember saying to myself, "I could be her friend." I was kind of sad thinking I wouldn't see you anymore. It sounds crazy but it's true.

And then came the man with the camera. I remember he just crouched in front of us, clicked, and walked away. I had no idea he was with a newspaper, because he just had a little Pentax or something. Later, I discovered his name was Jack Manning and was on staff at the *New York Times* and that was just how he worked, with very little equipment and very few shots. He didn't take many, but he took this one! If it wasn't for that sign, he would not have taken our picture. You and I are sitting here because of the sign.

By the way, the picture wasn't taken at the Paramount, as noted in the *Times*'s caption. Our photo was taken in daylight and the theater event was in the evening of the same day.

YEARS LATER I saw Paul McCartney on the street in Manhattan. That was *really* wild. I was nineteen at the time. I was on Fifth Avenue. I worked on Sixth Avenue at Lowenstein Fabrics; I was on my lunch break. I was crossing Fifth and he was approaching the same corner that I was coming to. My heart was pounding! He had married Linda and they were with her daughter Heather. I was very shy at the time but I knew I had to say something. There was no way I was not saying something.

When we met at the corner, we made eye contact and I said, "Congratulations," because they had just gotten married. He said, "Thank you 'veddy' much," just the way he does. And the little girl looked up and said, "Do we know her?" She was looking at me like . . . who are you? He said, "Yes, don't you remember?" He was making up a little story. It was so sweet. It was something like, "Don't you remember when we . . ."

I stayed back to see people's reactions as they walked by. People were asking each other, "Was that Paul McCartney? Was that Paul McCartney?" It was really quite a thrill. I immediately went to a phone booth and called my boyfriend. It was exciting, really wild, but it could have been George. If it had been, I don't know what I would have done.

EACH TIME I tell the story of how I found you and the famous photo, I'm amazed at the whole thing again. It's so surreal to me, the way it happened. The odds were so against it. I don't subscribe to *Vogue*. Sometimes my cousin will say, "Take this," and give me a copy, but that didn't happen all the time. And I'm not like a fashionista, although I did study fashion illustration many moons ago at the High School of Art & Design. I can't afford *Vogue*-wear.

I look at the magazine just to see what I will *not* be wearing. I always look at it from the back. I read it from back to front. I don't get into it that far. Once the editorials and ads start, I just leave it, I throw it away. I don't waste time on it.

After I saw the picture that night, that story went viral with people around here. My son called me for some other reason, I said, "David, I'm in *Vogue* magazine." He said, "I'll be right home." All of a sudden I was kinda cool. When I showed it to my cousin, who had given me the magazine, she was angry that she hadn't noticed it first. She was disappointed that she couldn't see my reaction to it. She said, "I used to see that picture all the time (in the *New York Times* and elsewhere) and I never even looked at it closely."

My long lost friend Joann was living in Arizona. I found her number, called her, and told her to get the magazine. I told her not to open it but to call me when she got it. I wanted to hear her scream. (She opened it anyway.) Then I wrote you a letter in care of *Vogue* but there was no reply. They obviously didn't forward it. About two years later, it clicked in my head to try to find you. I searched for you on Facebook and there you were.

By the way, you, Joann, Linda, and I are in the Scorsese film about George. We're right there in the street. You can see the sign, BEATLES PLEASE STAY HERE 4-EVER. I'm fiddling with my camera, scrooched down so you can't see my face. You and Joann are both facing the camera.

I had a suitcase full of memorabilia: ticket stubs, buttons, magazines, pieces of towels from the Plaza Hotel (guaranteed to have been used by them . . . LOL), things like that, all kinds of things. Many years later I asked my mother for the suitcase but she had thrown it away. . . . A suitcase full of memorable treasures, gone! I would love to see that stuff now.

It was when I saw *A Hard Day's Night* in 1964 that I really saw their "true" personalities come alive. It was then that I felt a stronger connection to George. It was something in his eyes. I felt as though I knew him, really knew him, as no one else could.

After watching the Scorsese film, I realized that, to this day, I still feel a connection, a certain affinity, with George, and I think I know why. He was a searcher. George was searching for God, and so was I.

America's Beatlemania Hangover
by Debbie Geller

AMERICA WAS STILL in mourning after the assassination of John Kennedy in November 1963. The nation was desperate for something entertaining and something light to replace the unrelenting presence of loss and grief. Then along came the Beatles, this breath of British fresh air and merriment, to charm and divert America back to mental health again. So the story goes.

I was much too young to know anything about national moods or historical trends when I sat down with my sisters to watch *The Ed Sullivan Show* that Sunday night. All I knew was that we were excited beyond reason and couldn't wait to see what *they* were really like. Apart from a few photographs, for most Americans, John, Paul, George and Ringo were pretty mysterious. So when they arrived in New York on February 7, there was pandemonium. It was a feeding-frenzy media circus—even if those were clichés yet to be invented.

In the few weeks leading up to the Beatles' arrival in New York, they had already transformed my life. And I'll always be grateful. We lived in Levittown, Long Island [New York], the archetype of American suburbia—the first step on the ladder for second-generation Americans on their way out of the decaying cities. Conformity and upward mobility were the most obvious features in the town. And it was no place for a left-wing, atheist, divorced family like ours. We were outcasts, treated more with suspicion than curiosity.

Within days of moving to our new home, I was asked by some of the neighborhood kids what religion we were. I had no idea of what they were talking about. I had never even heard the word before. This show of ignorance was greeted by hilarity and frustration. One girl finally begged me to just say anything. It didn't matter what we were, we just had to be *something*. But I wasn't able to indulge even that simple request. The role of local freak was given to us as a freehold. I wasn't so much bullied as barely tolerated.

But then a girlish democracy was created with the arrival of the Beatles. The old nasty prejudices suddenly melted away. Girls who had once teased and mocked me for everything from bad hair to reading too much were suddenly curious to know which Beatle I liked best. Life was getting easier. So when the curtain came up on *The Ed Sullivan Show* and the unusually animated host introduced "these youngsters from Liverpool" to a cacophony of screams, I already loved them. They were my ticket to acceptance and all the normal pleasures of being young.

It is hard to describe how fresh and delightful they looked that night—so eager to please and so pleased with themselves in a way that was completely guileless. When they sang "Till There Was You," the boys were introduced by name. White captions appeared under each face to distinguish Paul from George and George from Ringo.

John was identified with the immortal tag line: "Sorry, girls, he's married," a phrase that's still popular today.

That's how I learned that the one I liked best was George. It wasn't Paul after all—what a revelation! During the postmortem at school the next morning, I announced my discovery with confidence. Although Paul was the undisputed favorite, my choice was accepted with respect. And no one ever made fun of me again.

THERE CAN NEVER be another television moment like that one again—not in this hundred-channel-plus world. Forty percent of this country will never watch the same program at the same time. That's what made this event so unusual and so memorable. Most shared national moments are bizarre, at their most benign. Usually they are tragic and traumatic. But the Beatles' first appearance on *Ed Sullivan* is the rare, probably unique exception. It is the one shining occasion when 73 million people enjoyed the same thing at the same time.

THIS HAS BEEN a freezing winter. It obviously wasn't this cold in the winter of 1964—you can tell by the photographs. No one then looks as cold as they have in New York these days. There is also a freeze in the air that wasn't there forty years ago. Candidates for president are talking about hope and promising to "take the country back." I would like more than anything to believe them, but cynicism and distrust seem like the only realistic responses to politicians' words.

And there are no artists to capture the imagination either,

no one whose vitality and talent transform the world around them. That's what the Beatles did on that unforgettable night. The old black-and-white familiar images of four English boys on a cheap-looking stage go beyond nostalgia. Instead, they're a heartbreaking reminder of how hard it will be to ever feel so optimistic again.

"Cousin Brucie" Morrow,
disc jockey

. . . .

IN 1962, WHEN I first started getting these records by a group called the Beatles, none of us really took it too seriously. We'd had music from overseas before, but nothing that would cause a sociological change like the Beatles did. So we didn't think about it much.

But then something started happening. We were watching what was going on in Europe, in Hamburg, and all the places this band was visiting. The Beatles were causing riots! This was wonderful, in a way, because we *needed* something to happen in music at that time. We needed something very special. The music and radio industries were getting kind of dull. *Nothing* exciting was happening in American music. It was getting flattened out. Music was just lying there. The attitude in corporate America was "if it ain't broke, don't fix it," and that's very wrong.

We needed new energy.

So when the Beatles came over, these four "moptops" from overseas, all heck broke loose.

The band didn't happen overnight. It was a pretty long process, at least several years. John Lennon and Paul McCartney grew up listening to American rock and roll, blues, rhythm and blues, and jazz. They loved our expression of music. They loved the Everly Brothers and Chuck Berry and Jerry Lee Lewis.

At first they were replicating American music, they hadn't developed their own style. Then they began taking that music, beginning with rock and roll, and refining it, adding new energy and excitement to it. They developed this over the years, and a new sound came out—this whole new British sound— based on American rock and roll. They refined it and they went wild.

Their music was important, but what was more important at that time, in our lives and in our society, is that we needed something to latch on to, we needed to smile. We weren't smiling too much. We had assassinations. The nation was really divided. Youth was divided against anybody over thirty. You remember the old expression "Don't trust anyone over thirty"?

The Beatles *really* helped to bring the music world, the American music industry, together. They started fixing it. Well, they sort of helped to bring *everybody* together.

MY CAREER AND the name Cousin Brucie were born many years before the Beatles. You can trace it back to probably '58 when I was on [New York radio station] WINS.

We had Elvis and the Everly Brothers and all the early, early rock and roll groups—like the Drifters. I was very involved with all of them. I did a lot of shows with them; for years I was involved with Palisades Park. So my career was developing, it was doing very, very well. Still, the Beatles were probably the most important thing that happened in my career. They gave it a tremendous surge, a tremendous surge.

Because of the power of the New York radio station where I worked, WABC—which we eventually called "WABeatlesC"—I was the disc jockey who got the Beatles records before anybody else. This was literally due to power—because of this fifty-thousand-watt clearance from the transmitter, record companies like EMI and Capitol would make sure I received the records first. The other radio stations in the rest of the country wouldn't get them till the next day.

When new Beatle records came out it was huge, huge. They would arrive in my office with an armed guard and a promotion man. It was kind of weird—the guard would have an attaché case, with the new record in it, handcuffed to his wrist. I had to promise not to play it until the next day.

AM radio, which preceded satellite radio, had an interesting physical characteristic: It bounced off of the ionosphere. If you remember your physical science, you'll recall that the ionosphere rises at night. As it got later, the AM radio signal would bounce. The higher the ionosphere layer, the farther I would reach; by nine o'clock, I was reaching forty states. That's how I got a national image.

When other radio stations and Beatlemaniacs found out that I had a new record, and that I was going to be playing it, they would record it. I'd play it on the air and suddenly Pittsburgh, say, would have it or Wisconsin or Chicago. They'd have it that same night, they'd tape it off the air. It got so crazy with people taping that every ten seconds I would announce

"Exclusive! Cousin Brucie Exclusive! Exclusive!" and it would completely obliterate the record. It was a terrible thing to do but the audience understood. We had to do it so nobody else would copy the record, especially our local competitors.

Whoever got a Beatle record exclusive first won the game. We got the highest ratings. We would always get them.

THE BEATLES HAD an amazing sociological influence. I don't think that when they came here they knew what they were going to cause.

Beatlemania was an amazing thing, not only for the music industry but for the clothing industry, television, and the news. People started changing the way they spoke, the way they wore their hair, the way they dressed. Everybody changed their attitudes and we suddenly all became Anglophiles. It was very funny.

I'll give you a cute example: A boy named Johnny would call me from the Bronx, and he'd say something like—this is before the Beatles came over, a couple of weeks—he'd say "Hey, Brucie, this is Johnny from the Bronx, I live on the Grand Concourse. Will you play a record for my girlfriend, Shirley? Play something by Chuck Berry, will ya? We love him."

About three weeks later this same young man would call and this is what happened: "Ello, is this his majesty Brucie? This is Sir Jonathan of the Grand Concourseshire in Bronxville, would you mind playing a record for me and me bird?"

That, by the way, is very true. It happened many times. Suddenly everybody developed English accents and we were excited about something and people started smiling again. So the Beatles gave us something tremendous. Tremendous! A big party, that's what they gave us.

OH SURE, I met the Beatles many times. If you listen to my shows on SiriusXM now, you hear a promo that says something like "Hi, this is John! This is George! This is Paul! This is Ringo! We love you, Cousin Brucie!" They did that promo for me and they used to call me all the time from their car— this was before cell phones, they had mobile car phones.

I was at the original thing, the press conference they did at Idlewild Airport (which had just been named, you know, Kennedy, JFK Airport). They came on my show several times.

Anytime they came to New York they would come over to me because WABC—WABeatlesC—was a major station here in the city and, as I say, when I was on at night I reached forty states. Before satellite radio, that was a big deal.

On their first visit, I was up at the Warwick Hotel where they were staying, waiting to broadcast a live interview from their suite. While they were entering the hotel, a crowd of girls surged at them from across the street. They'd been herded behind police barricades at the Hilton Hotel but, when the Beatles came in by limousine, they broke through the barricades and came running to grab ahold of their heroes. They ripped Paul's hair and grabbed John's clothing and a certain young lady got hold of Ringo.

When the Beatles finally made their way upstairs, I said to

Ringo, "What's the matter? You don't look good." He said, "Somebody grabbed me St. Christopher's medal," and then I went on the air right away.

Of course, I knew I had something very important—if you got anything like that exclusively from the Beatles, it gave you a terrific winning possibility for ratings.

There were five or six thousand kids standing outside the hotel with their transistor radios. If I'd go over to a Venetian blind that was facing the kids, or even just say on the air something like, "Ringo, why don't you or Paul or John go look through the window at the kids"—you'd hear the kids [imitates a roaring sound] go crazy. All you had to do was shake the Venetian blind.

I went on the air and said to the kids: "Look, somebody must have found Ringo Starr's St. Christopher medal." I didn't say "took it" or "stole it." I said "somebody found it."

I said, "Look, if you return it you will not be in trouble and you'll come up here with Cousin Brucie and you'll meet Ringo and he'll give you a kiss." Well, of course the place went crazy, you heard them outside—W A A A G H!—through the windows. There were thousands of them.

When I got off the air a Mrs. McGowen called me. She said, "Cousin Brucie, my name is Mrs. McGowen and my daughter, Angela, found Ringo's St. Christopher medal." Of course she ripped it off his neck, we all knew that, but "she found it," her mother said.

"Is she in any trouble?" she asked.

I said, "No, on the contrary, she's going to be a very big hero in the newspapers and television and radio because she 'found' the St. Christopher medal."

I knew right away that I had a tremendous news piece and I didn't want anybody else to get it.

I said, "I would like you to stay right where you are, I'm going to send a car for you." So I sent a car for them and I sequestered them at the Hilton Hotel. That night I had my security guards from WABeatlesC get the girl and bring her back to me at the hotel. A huge number of press corps were there, television, radio, movies, you name it, all in that room, and Ringo and myself.

If you go onto the Internet, you can see the whole thing. The young lady was there with her friends and she got a kiss and Ringo got his St. Christopher's medal. To this day he remembers that medal and how I found it for him.

I INTRODUCED THE Beatles at Shea Stadium with Ed Sullivan—that was a very important part of my career. The Beatles were in the dugout at Shea and they were very nervous because there were sixty-five thousand screaming kids. You could feel the cacophony, the pressure of the emotion of the place.

John Lennon said to me, "Cuzzin"—he used to call me "Cuzzin"—"is this dangerous?" and I said, "No. John, let me tell you something. They're there for one reason, to share space with you. This is love, you're hearing love, emotional love, they just want to see you." Of course I wasn't too sure what was going to happen because it *was* a dangerous situation.

On the way up to the stage Ed Sullivan was in front of me. He was a real square fellow. He didn't really even know what the Beatles were, very honestly. He didn't know their power.

So he turns to me and says, "Is this dangerous, Cousin Brucie?"

I looked at him with his eyes bulging and I wanted to get him. I just knew I had him. And I said, "Yes, Ed, very."

He said, "It is? Very?"

And then he goes up another step. I follow, and he says, "What do we do?"

I thought to myself *I got him!*

To him I said, "Ed, pray!"

And he asked, "Pray?" He got so scared.

Anyway, to make a long story shorter, we went up there. I introduced Ed, he introduced the Beatles. Nothing happened of any disastrous nature that day. The police asked me to patrol with them and I went around Shea Stadium with them, calming everybody down and talking to them. The police were great.

So nothing really bad happened, everybody was contained and they were there, as I've said, with huge emotional love. There was so much energy—and this is something I love to say—that Con Edison, our public utility, could have turned off their turbines and electricity *still* would have been delivered to New York City because of the emotion and the energy.

As for the screaming girls, it was historic, you know? Why they did it is really a great psychological question. I've talked to shrinks about it, psychologists about it. We all need heroes.

And people tend to be very emotional. Now boys, unfortunately for them, they hold it in, they don't get as crazy outwardly emotionally. They hold their emotions in.

Women, young girls especially, have a capacity to let their emotions flow. And it's good, because they release it, and that releases tremendous energy. When they have somebody they love, they build up this pressure and they release it. Men do not do that too often.

AS FOR THE so-called rivalry between [WINS disc jockey] Murray the K and me, first of all, he's gone. He passed away many years ago. He had a terrible end to his life, so it's kind of tough to even talk about him.

He called himself "the Fifth Beatle," and honestly the Beatles did not like that. In many places in the country, in a lot of major markets, there was always a Fifth Beatle. So he hung on to that because he knew it would be a good thing for his career. But it was not official and it was not accepted or appreciated by the Beatles.

I *never* did that. Never did that, never claimed it. I was just there with them and we had a great time. They appreciated what I did for them and I appreciated them because they really saved the music industry. But that Fifth Beatle thing was nonsense.

I SPEAK TO Paul when he comes to town, he'll make an appearance on my SiriusXM radio show. So does Ringo. They come on and, you know, we talk and they either come up live or they call me on the telephone.

Paul is a warm, loving human being. He's a guy who says "Give me a hug." He's a terrific guy! I'll keep calling him "Sir Paul" to his face—I have such a respect for him. But he stops me, saying, "Brucie, it's *Paul.*" Ringo's the same way. They're both terrific guys.

It was an amazing time and I'm glad that I went through it. There are not actually too many people left who actually felt this amazing energy like I did, and I'm very appreciative.

I was very lucky. I consider myself lucky that I was here at the right time and at the right place because that's what this is all about. The Beatles were also at the right time and at the right place. And the audience? Well, they were, too. So we're all very lucky.

There'll never be another group that gains so much in so little time—by the way, it was only seven, eight years. They had such a huge, international audience! It was just one of those things. We needed it and they had it and they gave it.

Sister Mary Paul McCartney
by Mary Norris

. . . .

"HEY, MARY!" MY brother Miles hollered from the living room. "Get in here and watch this. These guys are going to be big." This group called the Beatles was on *Ed Sullivan*. I sat cross-legged on the floor in front of the TV. It was a big old cabinet model with a nick in the Bakelite rim from the time I crashed into it and chipped my tooth while trying to keep a balloon up in the air. I was twelve years old, and in sixth grade at St. Thomas More School.

Miles, who was five years older than me, was always trying to propel me to the next level. "You're still playing with paper dolls?" he had said, catching me in the garage with my girlfriends. "You should be listening to the radio and buying singles."

I was skeptical, but the next day at school every girl in the class had metamorphosed overnight into a full-blown Beatles fan. Even my dorkiest classmates had buttons—"I love Ringo" or "I love George"—pinned to the bibs of their uniforms. Irene, the most precocious girl in the class, had a Beatles button so big that it covered her entire chest, like a shield. I came home from school an avowed Beatles fan. My favorite was Paul.

Miles said that John was the obvious genius, but I stuck

with Paul. I soon knew everything about him that it was possible to know. He was sweet and innocent-looking, and had
the best voice, and was left-handed and motherless. There
was a problem, though. Well, maybe a few problems. There
was the age difference: he was ten years older than me, and I
couldn't get married until I was at least eighteen. Meanwhile,
he had a girlfriend, a red-haired actress named Jane Asher. (I
knew all about her, too. She had played Lady Jane Grey in *The
Prince and the Pauper*.) More worrisome was his religion. I had
heard on the radio, in an interview with George's sister, that
Paul was Church of England. I was steeped in Catholicism,
and couldn't imagine a future with Paul unless he converted.
So I folded my obsession with Paul McCartney into the litur-
gical year.

My mother had given me a five-year diary, a small brown
volume with a fleur-de-lis motif on the cover, noticeably absent
a lock and key. (Was she trying to keep tabs on me?) Digging
it out recently, I was impressed not so much by the prose quality ("Lousy day. It rained and ruined the first snow"), or even
by the enterprise and diligence that marked my early teens (I
have never been as busy as I was when I was in eighth grade),
as by the sheer fact that I wrote in it faithfully, four lines a day
for five years.

I had no idea what an oddball I was. While I thought I was
going forward as a wholesome teenager of my generation—
black-and-white houndstooth skirt, green fake-leather jacket—
I was actually backpedalling furiously into something like a
perpetual girlhood.

January 18, 1965—I made it to Mass and I'm glad, because this is supposed to be an octave of prayer, ending with the Conversion of St. Paul! Y'know what that means! I hope I can convert Paul! This is a perfect chance!

January 25, 1965—(Feast of the Conversion of St. Paul) Nothing happened yet. Testa wrote in my math book, "Roses are red 'vilets' are blue sugar is sweet so I love you. stuff that in your Pipe and smoke it." Wow! He's okay but I prefer Paul McCartney.

Paul Testa was the ugliest, baddest kid in class—fat, gap-toothed, crazy eyes, greasy hair—but if he really liked me I would be tempted to reciprocate. I was fat and self-conscious, but hopeful that someone would see my inner beauty. Every night, after kneeling beside my bed to write in my diary (naturally, I kept it under the mattress), I would will myself to dream about Paul McCartney. The closest I came to an erotic fantasy was picturing Paul behind me in line at the Dairy Queen.

I truly believed that God heard my prayers. I had lavished on my mother a spiritual bouquet—the promise of hundreds of rosaries and dozens of Masses—and I was deep in spiritual debt. The very day after I switched back to praying for her instead of Paul, a potential buyer appeared for our old house, a family property that my father had been trying to unload for years. Now I could concentrate on Paul with a clean conscience. I scoured the meager resources available to me—the Cleveland papers, *Time*, *16 Magazine*—looking for some item about Paul

McCartney, some sign from God that He would advance my special intention. A year later, I was still at it:

> January 24, 1966—Mon. Tomorrow's the conversion of St. Paul. Gosh, but I'm gonna pray!

The high-water mark of my twin obsessions came in the summer of 1966. I was in eighth grade, verging on fourteen, and the Sisters of the Incarnate Word were doing their best to funnel us girls into Catholic high schools. Sister Andrew had chosen my best friend, Mary Jo, and me to be on a panel about vocations. "Religious, that is!" I wrote (February 1, 1966). "Sister thinks I'm interested in a religious vocation." The thing that appealed to me most about being a nun was getting to change my name. The main thing that worried me was having to get up early in the morning. But I had an idea that I might be popular in the convent. In the outside world, or at a public high school, I would have to dress up and try to attract boys, but in the convent, or for the next four years at an all-girls school, I could avoid all that.

"If I'm ever a nun I'll be named after St. Paul," I wrote. "I'll only be a nun if I don't marry Paul." I liked the name Sister Mary St. Paul. My father's middle name was Paul, so no one would suspect that I was actually taking the name of Paul McCartney, the guardianship of whose soul would occupy me for eternity. (It wasn't until decades later that I began to suspect that Paul and the convent were smokescreens. The man I was really dedicated to, and didn't know how to let go of, was my father.)

That spring I was engaged in a protracted battle with Dad

to let me go to Lourdes Academy, a Catholic girls' school where all my friends were going: Mary Jo, Patsy, Connie, and even Irene, in her coveted John Lennon cap. Dad didn't want to pay tuition if he could send me to school for free, and he didn't want his daughter to be a churchy girl. He had refused to let me study Latin in a special Saturday class when I was in fifth grade, and when my piano teacher suggested I train to be a church organist, he said, "No dice."

On a spring day in 1966, secular and religious events converged to lift my spirits:

> March 17, 1966—Happy Saint Patrick's Day! We went to Mass at the Cathedral & Bishop Elwell gave me Communion. That ring! . . . The parade was great. Dad said hi to us. [We were Irish, of course. Dad marched with the fire department.] And Locher lifted the Beatle ban!

Ralph Locher, the mayor of Cleveland, had banned the Beatles after their first tour, in 1964, when fans had stormed the stage at Public Auditorium. I didn't go—even if I had been able to scrape up $7.50 for a ticket, my father would never have let me go downtown alone at night. Irene had gone, but her father was dead.

On Tuesday, May 3, 1966, it was announced that the Beatles were coming back to Cleveland and would play at the stadium on August 14. That the concert fell on a Sunday was auspicious: maybe Paul would come to the eleven-fifteen Mass at Thomas More!

As graduation approached, my father relented and said I

could go to Lourdes. The nuns had given me a scholarship, which demolished his argument about the tuition.

My diary reflects my excitement as both of my projects shifted into high gear:

May 4, 1966—Weds. Sister thinks I'm gonna be a nun. How am I supposed to know?! Two nuns congratulated me on the scholarship. Me, Connie, & Mary Jo finally talked to Sister tonight. She's great!

May 8, 1966—Sun. We went for a ride & that was fun. I'm trying to win Beatle tickets. I've got to go! I'm really gonna go on a diet & get pretty & meet Paul this summer.

The tickets were going on sale at the stadium at nine o'clock in the morning on Saturday, May 21. My best friend, Patsy, was going to stay overnight at my house the Friday before, and we would get up early and take the bus downtown. My parents didn't encourage us to invite friends to stay overnight, or let us stay overnight at our friends' houses, a policy I never understood. Anyway, I finagled it—caught Dad in a good mood and framed it so it made financial sense.

That Friday night, Dad took us all out to dinner at the Flat Iron Café, in the Flats. The special was a fish fry. I hated fish (it would be a year before Catholics were no longer compelled to eat fish on Friday) and was relieved that I could have macaroni-and-cheese. My mother said, "I had to tee-hee when I thought of that Patsy telling her father we took her to a beer joint." My father was at his most gracious. After dinner, he gave us a tour of the bridges over the Cuyahoga River.

May 21, 1966—Sat. I'm dead tired. Stood out in the pouring rain for over 5 hours. Got a ticket, though. I think I'll be on Paul's side.

Patsy and I got seats in the lower deck: Section 27, Row 10, Seats 16 and 17. I was familiar with the stadium, because I was a baseball fan—the old stadium was huge, and the Cleveland Indians, those perennial losers, could never fill it up; the Cleveland *Press* gave free tickets to anyone who got straight A's—so I knew that our seats were on the left-field side.

Irene was way ahead of us in line—she had been there all night. (She called herself Rinny now, and she had given a British name to her dog, Geoff, which we all, Irene included, pronounced in what we thought was the British way: GEE-off.) Her seat was probably down on the field.

Thus began the long vigil:

May 22, 1966—Sun. . . . Can't wait till Aug. 14!

June 5, 1966—Sun. The Beatles were on Ed Sullivan. They were OK, but they should've changed the order of songs & should've not worn those dopey glasses. Paul looked sweet but like he chipped his tooth.

June 17, 1966—It's Paul's birthday right now & I heard that he bought himself (as a birthday present, the dope!) a farm in Scotland. Man, would I love that!

July 3, 1966—Sun. . . . Finished a letter to Paul which is pretty good.

July 9, 1966—Sat. Took a bath & the works & I'm gonna
be different tomorrow. Skinny! We've been sorta mad at
Connie lately, but who cares. I've got to get a job. And I've
got to meet the Beatles.

July 19, 1966—Tues. Jinxed the Indians. They lost. . . .
Race riots on the east side. Civil War II on the way.

World events rarely intruded into my diary (I allotted half
a line to the death of Winston Churchill), but my father's
fire station was on the East Side, and that summer, when his
company responded to an alarm in the Hough district, rioters
threw bricks and stones at the firemen.

Dad was already a bigot, and now he was mad. Downtown
Cleveland was about halfway between where we lived—on
the West Side, near the zoo—and the slums. Downtown was
black. I knew that Dad would give me a hard time about being
there at night after the concert.

Then an earth-shattering revelation:

July 20, 1966—Wed. Paul really did chip his tooth!
What'd I tell you! I love him more than ever! And I'm
gonna write him a letter & tell him so! He flipped off
his motorbike & had to get stitches in the mouth! Sweet.

July 21, 1966—Thurs. . . . Wrote Paul a letter. I keep
thinking about his tooth!

The chipped tooth was a big deal to me. I had been devastated when I chipped my own tooth against the TV that time.

I'd never seen a Miss America contestant with a chipped tooth, so there went that fantasy. My mother took me to our ancient dentist, but he declined to cap it or do anything cosmetic. (Electroplating, if it had been invented, was not in his repertoire.) "But I can't go through life like this!" I wailed. "Oh, I think you can," the dentist said.

> July 26, 1966—Tues. Went swimming. I am too darn fat! I'll never make a hit with Paul. (I love his tooth!) Mary Jo got a postcard from Sr. Andrew. Gotta brush my hair.

Around August 4, John Lennon made his famous remark about the Beatles' being bigger than Jesus Christ, and the Beatles were banned in the Bible Belt. The furor soon died down, but the fact that religion had come up during the Beatles' tour gave me new hope as Paul set out on the road to Cleveland. I boldly committed to my diary my most fervent desire. "I wish Paul would tell him off, the Beatles would break up, & Paul would enter a seminary," I wrote. "Now you know!"

The next ten days were a frenzy of devotion. I listened to the radio religiously. Paul won a Favorite Beatle Contest, beating John by five hundred votes. My favorite disc jockey, Jerry G, was going to interview him when he was in Cleveland. *Revolver* came out, and "Eleanor Rigby" was issued as a single, with "Yellow Submarine" on the flip side. I watched for sightings of Paul on the news, redid my bedroom door with fresh pictures of my one and only, babysat to earn money to buy film and flashcubes to take pictures at the concert. My father would be working that night, and if there were no fires or riots he was going to pick Patsy and me up in the chief's car and drive us home. The chief's car could get through anything.

August 13, 1966—Sat. Made $3 at Aber's house. Nice people & kids! You know what tomorrow is! I can't wait! Paul is gonna sing "Yesterday." I'm gonna stay up all night reading & waiting for the Beatles' arrival & writing Paul a letter!

Certain that Paul would be feeling hemmed in by the constant travel and the strain of being on tour, I invited him to dinner. If Jesus Christ could rise from the dead, Paul McCartney could come to Sunday dinner, and my mother could put something decent on the table. Chatty and confidential—I felt free to be myself with Paul—I gave him precise directions.

All he'd have to do was catch the 81 bus on Prospect Avenue, across the street kitty-corner from Public Square. The bus stop was in front of a lingerie store called Mamselle, which was next to a nut shop that sold roasted cashews. He would need correct change. I apologized to Paul for the dreary route. Sometimes it seemed to me that the 81 took the longest possible route to our neighborhood, covering every street on the West Side that wasn't served by some other bus. Scranton, Storer . . . I dreaded to think of Paul on these soulless thoroughfares. But I wanted him to see the real Cleveland.

I explained to him how the boring part would be over once the bus had made a major right turn onto Denison, and then a quick left onto Ridge. He'd pass Zayre's on the left, where I shopped for fabric; a doughnut shop in the shape of a crown;

and a bowling alley, where my first bowling score had been a humiliating nineteen (lots of gutter balls). Coming up on the left was a storage facility for telephone poles (it reeked of creosote), and then he should watch on the right for Merhaut Flowers and pull the cord to let the driver know he was getting off. Our stop was on the far side of the green bridge: Orchard Grove. He'd have to cross Ridge and walk up one block, to the Phillips 66 station, then turn left onto Meadowbrook. We were the seventh house on the right, a white colonial with green shutters. We ate at six.

I knew what hotel they were staying in. Perhaps I could hand the letter to a policeman to pass along to Paul?

On the evening of the concert, Patsy and I dressed in our Sunday best. I had on a panty girdle and my Easter outfit (without the hat and white gloves). I had the letter in my purse, along with my ticket, my Brownie camera, and a dime to call my father.

Revolver was playing—"For No One"—as we found our seats. The stage was on the pitcher's mound, impossibly far away, but the girl next to me let me use her binoculars, and for one ecstatic moment they brought me right up to Paul McCartney's feet.

I rarely exceeded the four lines provided for an entry in my diary, but on this occasion I spilled over into 1967:

August 14, 1966—Sun. Wild scene! 5,000 kids, I was almost one of them, stormed the stage & the show was stopped. It was terrific, though! They had dark green suits & yellowish-green shirts. Paul was lovely. He sang

"Yesterday" & almost everyone shut up! He waved & everything & stood behind a pole! We were far away, but in some girl's binoculars he was close-up & man is he a doll!

When everyone stormed the stage, Patsy turned to me and said, "Should we go?" "I don't know," I said, staring straight ahead. I had turned into a pillar of salt. We stood at our assigned seats as everyone around us surged forward. That night, I later read, John Lennon said backstage that this would be their last tour.

> August 15, 1966—Mon. Paul has a black kitten with white whiskers, with a real cool name, which I couldn't understand. He is so funny. I wish I could sit around all week in solitude listening to Jerry G interviewing him. They left at 2 PM.

I failed to note that August 15 was the Feast of the Assumption of the Blessed Virgin Mary into Heaven. It did not escape my notice that Paul McCartney had been hustled out of town before dinnertime.

A FEW DAYS later, I got a letter from Sister Andrew. She had been transferred, and Mary Jo and I made plans to visit her at the new convent. Paul got his tooth capped. My pictures didn't come out—all I got was the backs of people's heads.

In January, Jerry G, my favorite disc jockey, left town. "I don't understand how anyone can call a city the best location in the nation & say its people are fantastic & they love it & it has captured them & then move to Chicago," I wrote, bitterly.

That year, Paul's Birthday, which I had given special holiday status in my diary, coincided with Father's Day.

June 18, 1967—Sun. Ed Sullivan wished Paul a happy birthday, but today ended rather strangely. Paul revealed that he has taken LSD four times this past year. He said it has brought him closer to God and made him a more honest man, but still I wish I were dreaming.

It was not the outcome I had been hoping for.

June 19, 1967—Mon. There was an article in the paper about Paul and LSD today. I think God has answered my prayers. Or at least started to. LSD was the means by which Paul has come close to God.

Psychedelic drugs were not the only development that took time to sink in. When I went back to school in the fall, the nuns were different. They had changed out of their habits and reverted to their baptismal names. Sister Mary Abram, my French teacher, became Sister Diane Branski, of the dimpled elbows; a few years later, she left the convent and started smoking and using hair spray and wearing makeup. Sister Mary Peyton, a.k.a. Pat Gaski, who had wide-spaced pale-blue eyes and was very athletic for a nun, whipping the long blue skirts of her robe around when she perched on a desktop, held out until the following spring, when we were aghast to see her in a sailor suit.

By the time I read about Paul McCartney's breakup with Jane Asher, his role in my life was greatly diminished. "I took all my Beatle magazines & Trixie Belden books downstairs," I recorded (August 31, 1968). "I'm going to save them for my posterity." One day, while I was away at college, my father cleaned the garage, where he had stashed the two big boxes that contained my archive, and threw them out. It made me sad.

It was over, of course. My determination to convert my idol had been absurd, misguided, laughable, naïve . . . but at the time it had served its purpose. You might even say that it was my salvation.

Anyway, that was the end of Sister Mary Paul McCartney.

Peter Duchin, bandleader

. . . .

I WAS PLAYING at the Maisonette in New York City in 1964 when the Beatles arrived on the scene. It was at the St. Regis Hotel and it was a very ritzy but wonderful place and all sorts of people came from all walks of life. People would dine, dance, and hopefully have a good time.

Whenever we would play a Beatles song, which we did often, old guys would come up and say "Good lord! What's that longhair music you're playing?" Because of the Beatles' hairdos they considered the music to be "longhair." It was really amusing.

I thought the Beatles sounded great, especially lyrically. Rhythmically they were up and down. It wasn't a group you necessarily looked at technically, perhaps because of the drummer, but they were really interesting lyrically. Many of the tunes were totally unlike the American songbook tunes we had been used to playing. Just look at a lyric like "Eleanor Rigby" or "Fool on the Hill"! People were not necessarily writing tunes about that kind of thing. It was all quite poetic and whimsical.

I began playing their music as soon as I started hearing it. Since we had to play every night, we not only played all the show tunes and old tunes and Cole Porter and all of that, but whatever was out there—Little Richard, the Beatles, et cetera. I played whatever I felt like playing, same as today.

There was other stuff, like Bo Diddley, that we played but that was not yet really accepted by society. The Beatles slowly became acceptable but it took a while for middle-aged people to actually let go and dance to that kind of music. The parents of a lot of the kids who really loved the Beatles couldn't understand the craze. They'd ask, "God, how can you listen to that stuff?"

It was the sixties and American culture was in for a rude shock. I well remember chuckling with the band as we watched older people trying to emulate the way their kids were dancing on the floor. They gave new meaning to the term *self-conscious*!

The Beatles were in Hamburg for what, two or three years? They had all that time there, playing with and listening to other groups, and they noticed that everybody played the same thing. They had to work out their own style. They started doing their own thing. They were so talented that they totally changed the face of popular music.

Their music is still wonderful. It allowed other things to happen that might not have happened. It certainly changed the face of the American songbook. And it allowed all sorts of groups—the Who, the Doors, endless other rock and roll groups that might not have been as adventurous—to happen. And that's important.

I think their lyrics tapped into feelings that were as yet unexpressed by the kids who were their fans. They represented the rebellion that was in the air back then.

Anne Brown, fan

· ·

WHEN I WAS going into about the eighth grade, we went and settled in Charleston, South Carolina, where all the rest of our family lived. Charleston was a very, very kept-back little town. It was a repressed little town to be a teenager in. It sure felt that way. Of course, probably all of America was then.

Charleston had its heyday and then it was very much in decline for many years—which is probably why it's so well preserved at this point. It didn't keep growing and bustling.

The whole Beatles thing that came washing over America barely touched South Carolina. The scene in Charleston was pretty calcified. Fresh new things, new thinking, anything like that was threatening and not welcome and not enjoyed. It was such an impenetrable place.

I first learned of the Beatles when I heard some of their songs on the radio. Their music was *totally* unusual down there. What played on local radio was something called "beach music," a kind of regional form of Motown. These were black singing groups—the Tams were one example—that were often made up of four guys, four women, that kind of thing. A dance called the shag, of all things, often went with beach music.

I saw all of the *Ed Sullivan* stuff from the very beginning.

I wasn't just flipping through the channels: I knew about the band, I knew some of their music. I don't know if I had a Beatles album at that point, I probably just got 45s for a while. At any rate, I was very primed to go down that road when they came on the show.

I must have been in the ninth grade when they came. I attended an all-girls school called Ashley Hall—it's still there. An all-girls school was wonderful for me. I liked hanging around with the smart, smart, smart girls.

In Charleston, you didn't have to be very risk taking to be rebellious. Walking around barefoot in public or having a little bit of a short skirt would do it. It wasn't hard to get a maverick sort of reputation.

By liking the Beatles we were definitely odd ducks. It was not as if their music ever became popular there. Just a handful of girls in my school—eight or nine of us—were what I would call Beatlemaniacs. I had a few friends, and we were not girls who were popular with boys, and we just all swerved off into this lane and had a great time for a few years, just being swept up and carried away and living in our own little club of a world.

Between the Beatles and the all-girls school, I didn't have to bother with boys at all. There wasn't a population of boys around me every day who could hurt my feelings by ignoring me. So that was gone. Plus, I was totally fascinated and wrapped up in these four other young men who were totally undangerous, so that was great.

From the point of view of conventional parents, conventional people, the Beatles were dangerous boys. They were nowhere near as nasty as Elvis was, though, not even close. I wasn't into Elvis, I was a little too young for that, but it was all that again—teen sex and teens running wild, all those fantasies of adults that were never really true.

THERE WERE SIXTY girls in my graduating class and, of those, about twenty were my cousins, second or third cousins. After the Beatles came to America, the parents of a third cousin in my grade were kind enough to take us to see them in concert, two years in a row. The first one was in Jacksonville, Florida, at the Gator Bowl; the second at the Peach Bowl in Atlanta.

They took about five of us and we had just a wonderful time. They let us just be crazy. They weren't worried about us, they pretty much gave us free rein.

The Gator Bowl was a lousy little stadium compared to what it must be now—it's been replaced, I'm sure. I guess we got there a day early. Our little motel was right next to the stadium and we crept around it that whole first day, scoping everything out. We were circling around underneath the bleachers when we came across a chain-link fence—I don't know if it was a permanent installation or not. And there was the Beatles' trailer just beyond it. It was so amazing!

We were the only girls down there, me and my friends, and we leaned on the fence and watched people come and go. We could just catch a glimpse of the Beatles, who must have been hanging out, drinking, and having a big old time.

There was a security guard there and we asked him to get

us an autograph. He knocked on the door and came back with something that he said was Paul McCartney's autograph and gave it to me. That night I didn't have anything to compare it with so I thought it was authentic. Over time, as I saw more and more of Paul's signature, I thought, "You know what? I don't think so." I think that security guard or somebody in the trailer just wanted to get rid of us.

Still, it was a wonderful concert. I think Dusty Springfield was the opening act and she was wonderful. But I was a screamer, a big screamer, and, between the screaming around me and the screaming that I was doing, I couldn't hear any of the music very well.

After the concert was over and the Beatles were swept off in a limo to their hotel, we girls stayed in the stadium and just crawled all over everything, investigating. I took handfuls of gravel from below the bottom step, where you'd get down from the stage—they had to have all stepped down there. I kept handfuls of that gravel in a Baggie for years. Then I went on the stage and pried up splinters from where each one of the Beatles had been standing and singing. I was careful to document which splinter belonged to which Beatle.

I got other funky things at the Gator Bowl concert, too. People still had flash cameras then and there were light bulbs around that trailer. I picked up a lot of them—they might been involved in taking a picture of one of them, you know. I was just scavenging, pawing at everything I could get. The gravel and the splinters were particularly exciting because they certainly had had contact with Beatle feet.

It was sweet, it really was, when I think back about it now. I just can't believe how sweet it was, really, to be so innocently occupied.

There seemed to be an innocence about the Beatles themselves, too, but that wasn't the case at all. The stuff that you hear now about what was going on with them when they were riding that highway was amazing. They were quite promiscuous and quite experimental and ingesting everything and they were not what they appeared to be. They did not want to hold your hand.

THE NEXT CONCERT, the one in Atlanta, was in a great big modern stadium for back then—bigger seats, bigger everything. Our seats weren't in the front row but close to it. There was a drop-off between them and the stage. I'm not sure how high it would have been.

I was so excited at that concert, but then I had a moment of thinking I couldn't hear them. I don't know what came over me. I got mad—and I just made the decision that I was going to charge the stage. Which is really not like me. At any rate, I made that decision.

I made my way down to the railing between the seating area and the stage and I just went over it. I hung on the rail, then I dropped, dropped down to the ground, maybe eight or ten feet. And then I got up and started running toward the stage.

This is the best moment of Beatlemania for me. There was this din going on all the time and, when the screaming girls saw somebody going across the field, it just went up. Way up. It got louder—I don't know how many decibels—and it gave me such a rush as I ran. I was just carried by that.

And then there were two policeman or security guards running toward me, running toward me, running toward me, and I managed to scoot right in between them and get away from them and there was even more screaming from the crowd. I managed to get to the stage—a kind of platform they'd put up—and throw myself up onto it. It was low, probably chest high. I dove onto the corner where John Lennon was, but the two security guys grabbed my feet and yanked me off right away.

They pulled me off and knocked the breath out of me so they had to give me some smelling salts. The show went on. The guards sort of pulled me around the back or something to give the smelling salts to me. I had waited until the end to make the run and it was the last song. The guards then escorted me out of the stadium, took me outside, and seemed to feel that I could find my parents and my ride on my own, which I could.

That was a big, big moment for me. I was as un-well-behaved as I could be without pushing things too far. It was great.

There was a little paragraph about it in one of the local papers that read, "Oh, and one girl, dah, dah, dah." It was a thrill, it really was.

When I threw myself on the stage I was closest to John at that point. It happened too fast. I was diving onto the stage, so my head was down. I wasn't able to look up and see the love in John's eyes. [Laughs] That didn't happen.

SHORTLY AFTER THAT the Beatles' music changed and I minded it a lot. It was probably *Revolver*. Wasn't that the first one that was a little different? A lot different. It was political, it was druggy, it was not hand-holding music. I got to like that music when I was older but I felt somewhat abandoned when I was younger, when I was at that age.

In the course of that two-year Beatlemaniac period, a friend of mine and I wrote a book about how we stowed away in some kind of shipping boat and ran away to England and met the Beatles and all fell in love with each other, and they married us, of course. We each wrote alternate chapters.

It's so funny, I came across it a few years ago and I just felt so tender for these little girls writing this book. I'm sure it's different now because we've all got the Internet and nobody can hold anybody back.

I do look back on it all in amazement and I remember that moment of being mad. That was funny, you know. It just seemed so pointless to be standing there, screaming with a bunch of girls. It sort of galvanized me to take action.

We were growing up. We were growing up.

A Diary Entry

by Anne Brown, age 15

— 59 —

afterthought —————

There one was only one thing that
I didn't was kind of disheartening
about the Beatles. For them it was
everyone in Jacksonville was getting
all excited and having a stroke
and all, while for the Beatles it
was just, to them, another day, and it
didn't mean a thing to them.
That is kind of depressering.

Springsteen's Hair Stands on End
by Peter Ames Carlin

· ·

IN EARLY 1964 Bruce was riding in the front seat of his mother's car when "I Want to Hold Your Hand" beamed out of the radio. "It's those old stories, like when you hear something and your hair stands on end," Bruce reminisced to [Steve] Van Zandt. "It's having some strange and voodoolike effect on you." Leaping out of the car, Bruce sprinted to a nearby bowling alley that he knew had a telephone booth, slammed his way into the box, and spun the number of the girl he was dating. *"Have you heard of the Beatles? Have you heard this song?"*

"It stopped your day when it hit," he said on Van Zandt's syndicated *Underground Garage* radio show in 2011. "Just the sound of it. And you didn't even know what they looked like." Then the Beatles were shaking their astonishing mops on *The Ed Sullivan Show,* and then they were dominating the radio dial, with a wave of similarly tressed countrymen marching on their Cuban boot heels. When summer came, Bruce invested a few weeks painting his aunt Dora's house, then used $18 of his proceeds to buy an acoustic guitar he'd seen in the window of the Western Auto store on Main Street. Next he bought himself a copy of the *100 Greatest American Folk Songs* songbook and committed himself to mastering the instrument.

FUN
by Véronique Vienne

. . . .

I WAS ON my way out the door when someone turned up the volume on the TV and I spun around. I couldn't see the screen—but there was this incredible sound coming from the tube. I can only compare it to the jingle of hundreds of slot machines splashing tokens into metal pans. Psychedelic tinnitus. Audible dopamine. The acoustical equivalent of vibrating synapses.

Fun.

Fun?

The deafening shrieks of teenage girls cheering the Beatles on *The Ed Sullivan Show* was a sound I couldn't identify or name. There is no equivalent for the word *fun* in my native language. I am French.

In February 1964, American women were flushing French perfume down the toilet because Charles de Gaulle, then president of France, had established diplomatic relations with communist China. I was new to Francophobia. I had come to New York to be with my boyfriend, a brilliant Yale graduate who, among other accomplishments, spoke French fluently. His mother was also a Francophile but her husband refused to acknowledge me or talk to me because he thought that I was a communist. As a student in a French Beaux Arts school, I had found an intern position with the legendary French designer Raymond Loewy, whose offices were in New York. My accent in English was atrocious. People only pretended to understand what I was talking about.

That spring, my boyfriend took me to visit a college friend of his, a trust-fund brat who lived in Greenwich Village and had perfected the raffish bohemian look of the moment. He showed us his most recent acquisition, a brand new Seeburg jukebox, and proposed to demonstrate how it worked by playing a couple of Beatles songs on it. But he didn't have the proper coins and neither did we. "Wait a minute," he said, "I'll go down to the corner deli and get some change." I was puzzled. He owned the instrument, so why did he have to pay to use it? Surely he could have tampered with the mechanism to avoid this inconvenience?

His answer blew me away.

"I put coins in the jukebox because it's fun," he said.

Fun. F.U.N.

Three letters that changed my life.

A couple of months later, de Gaulle criticized the U.S. involvement in Vietnam. Americans expressed their anti-French feelings by pouring Bordeaux wine and Champagne down the drain. Confused, I speculated that it must have been "fun" to uncork the bottles and empty their content into a yawning porcelain bowl. Then I was on a roll. The word fun helped me to characterize my whole New York experience: sitting at a drugstore lunch counter, drinking soda pop from the bottle, double-dating, or pinning a corsage on my winter coat.

But I was faking it. There was a dimension of mirth I could never achieve. It was there in the intoxicating din of fans cheering the Beatles, in their jubilation and revelry. It was there in their childish delight and the abandon with which they expressed it. Years later, when the term "baby boomers" was coined, I assumed that it described the booming voices I had heard that night on *The Ed Sullivan Show*—an upsurge of optimism triggered by the sight of the baby-faced performers.

I am not a boomer. I am four years ahead of the celebrated demographic bulge. My daughter, born is 1968, also missed being part of that same prestigious cohort—1964 being the last year on your birth certificate to qualify as a boomer. Although she and I sometimes pass for boomers (we have our moments of levity), neither of us is endowed with the natural exuberance that is the birthright of the 78.3 million Americans born in the post–World War II era.

Looking back, I can say in all earnest that acquiring that glee has been something of a spiritual quest.

It all started on February 9, 1964, at 8:10 p.m. EST, to be precise.

WHY ARE SOME defining moments fixed forever in our mind, while others slip by, only to be revived, like Proust's madeleine, in the glory of our hindsight? When I stood in the doorway of my boyfriend's parents' bedroom, listening to the loud screeching and screaming that punctuated every chord of "All My Loving," how did I know that this particular scene deserved the Madame Tussaud's treatment?

Today, I am revisiting the posh bedroom in this luxury New York co-op apartment as if I were on a 3D virtual tour. The décor is faux Italian Renaissance, with a built-in wall unit as ornate as the façade of a Venetian palace, complete with rows of loggias, one of which houses the bulky black-and-white television. A middle-aged woman wearing pearls and a quilted turquoise dressing gown reclines on the king-size bed, a cigarette in her bejeweled hand. Her husband, a monumental presence in a regal silk robe, stands by the window, a look of disbelief on his face. They have been stuck there, this prosperous pair, captive in my mind, for about fifty years. In the process, they have acquired a waxy, oily sheen.

I look around for clues. Everything in the room is monogrammed, gold-plated, marbleized, floor-length, wall-to-wall, special-ordered, embellished, tailor-made, custom-built, five-star, certified, and hand-finished. This claustrophobic environment is what affluence looked like in America in the early sixties—in bedrooms such as this more than a few boomers were conceived.

Not just a tableau, this memory is an installation. The black-and-white TV has been broadcasting the same program all these years. The image on the screen flickers as the kids keep screaming.

This is my ground zero. My quest will start right here, on the twenty-first floor of this luxury co-op, overlooking the East River, with the Triborough Bridge in the distance.

That evening my boyfriend and I snuck away from his parents' bedroom, leaving them to their televised bewilderment.

It was snowing. The doorman called us a cab and we headed crosstown through Central Park to the railroad flat I shared with a roommate on West 72nd Street. I slept in an alcove in the living room, while she was ensconced in the bedroom. Her boyfriend was a rowdy character, while my boyfriend was a typical Ivy Leaguer, herringbone tweed jacket, penny loafers, and all. He had recently become my lover—if you can call love the fumbling that usually preceded the debacle in the alcove.

But my preppy ejaculator was a hunk. His torso was an armored plate. His pelvic bones, cresting on either side of his taut belly, were strung like a Celtic harp. His arms and legs were wreaths of muscle. He may have been a Sistine Chapel specimen, but he was a disappointment in the sack. Even so, the intimacy between us could be thrilling. We would huddle and giggle under the blanket as stark naked figures emerging from my roommate's bedroom made frequent beelines for the refrigerator, jerking it open in search of liquid sustenance.

Bad sex has redeeming qualities. Bad sex can be fun. Never underestimate the pleasure of crumpling sheets, spilling wine on the carpet, and mucking up towels. My boyfriend, alas, did not appreciate such simple delights. An inspired wordsmith who eventually got a doctorate in art history, he could enthuse about abstract expressionist smears and smudges—and would later do so in a five-hundred-page volume about modern art—yet he never saw the beauty of our more sultry drips and splotches.

The Rolling Stones album *Sticky Fingers*, released in 1971, was a far cry from the Beatles' early hit "I Want to Hold Your

Hand." Its message was clear: there's more to sex than the missionary position. But for my boyfriend and me that news came too late. We had married each other, become parents, and engaged in extramarital sex, all without ever finding our way, sexually, to the viscous and molten center of the earth.

NEVER HAD THE gap between one generation and the next been so painfully acute. On one side were such plain-vanilla kids as my boyfriend and me, utopians whose values were rooted in mid-century aesthetics; on the other side was a fun-loving cohort of Pop Culture savants whose appetite for commercial trivia became a permanent feature of the American psyche. In 1964, Warhol, Lichtenstein, and Jasper Johns mounted the American Supermarket exhibition, an event that turned Campbell's soup cans into a national symbol. Warhol was a buffoon of sorts, but so was my boss at the time, Raymond Loewy, a trendsetter at the opposite end of the fun spectrum.

Loewy had always been the laughingstock of the New York design establishment. The people at MoMA simply dismissed him as a "stylist." When I met him, he was a debonair little Frenchman, with a sedate smile, manicured hands, and a middle-age spread. At the end of the day he would tour the bullpen (the room was the size of a city block), silently reviewing the work of the different designers. No one spoke. He would take out his fancy fountain pen and sign with a flourish a couple of drawings before moving on. The remainders were emphatically thrown away—without his autograph, they were worthless.

When I got there, my professional ambition, nourished by

Bauhaus delusions, had been to design politically correct electric fans and alarm clocks. Industrial design was a calling, as far as I was concerned. But Loewy was not Walter Gropius, far from it. Known for his streamlined locomotives and slenderized kitchen appliances, he would put whoosh lines and speed whiskers on everything from iceboxes to toothbrushes.

While I had hoped to work on something modernistic, perhaps an aerodynamic lemon squeezer or torpedo-shaped cups and saucers, I was in for a reality check. My first assignment was to draw a twelve-foot-long malignant cell. The giant protoplasm was to be the centerpiece of an exhibit for the American Cancer Society, an educational installation in the Hall of Science at the New York World's Fair.

It should look like something from outer space, I was told. Light it from behind to make it glow.

Seriously? Indeed.

While the official theme of the 1964 New York World's Fair was "Peace through Understanding," it was actually designed to glorify commercial messages—it had the dubious distinction of being the first international exposition to give consumer brands the same status as participating nations. Conceived as a huge amusement park, with 200 major American corporations, such as Westinghouse, Clairol, General Foods and Simmons, it was a square mile of sideshows, live demonstrations, interactive exhibits, and fun rides. Its product-as-entertainment strategy targeted young consumers—the same teens who had shrieked through *The Ed Sullivan Show*. Millions of them came, accompanied by their parents.

My sci-fi cancer cell wasn't exactly "fun"—I labored over graphic displays dramatizing cervical cancer and the lifesaving wonders of the Pap test—but it was part of the same insidious scheme. The American Cancer Society had, for all intents and purposes, been transformed into a consumer brand.

THE WORLD'S FAIR—NICKNAMED the "laissez-fair"—was the ugliest urban sprawl I had ever seen. Yet it was "fun!" Every visitor could find something to love amid the bric-a-brac of pavilions, reflective pools, memorials, and archways, even though waiting in line to see the shows—GM's Futurama, Westinghouse's time capsule, Clairol's hair-coloring carousel—was usually the most thrilling part of the experience.

It was the same with the Beatles. The band was fun because it offered something for everyone. "Who's your favorite Beatle?" was the burning question. Each one of the four musicians was so different—you almost *had* to love him more than the others. For me it was Ringo. Of course! In my estimation, the other three only existed to better showcase the quirky charm of the drummer.

As long as each performer had his own following—and each fan could demonstrate his or her allegiance with impunity—the popularity of the group was assured. To their bitter end, the Beatles preserved the public's right to choose one over the other. In so doing, they confirmed the fragile individuality of each and every one of their screaming fans, a strategy that made Beatlemania that much more fulfilling and buoyant.

Contrary to popular belief, fun is not a shared experience. It is a very private emotion, an internal simmering of delicious apprehensions. Though it may express itself in a boisterous display of glee, it never loses its quiet, confidential dimension.

At the World's Fair, I made a discovery whose memory outshines all others. Thinking about it provokes in me a Cheshire-Cat grin. What generated my merriment was "Think," a short multiscreen projection sponsored by IBM for its World's Fair pavilion. The strange and marvelous theater, designed by Eero Saarinen, in which this event took place resembled a giant egg resting on a canopy of steel trees. The show itself consisted of fifteen films by Charles and Ray Eames that, projected together, deliberately stimulated and challenged the viewer's cognitive faculties.

Under the pretext of comparing the logic of computers with that of human beings, the Eameses created an exquisite visual choreography that got you to feel—and actually be—smarter. Juxtaposing signs and images into an ever-changing pattern, they turned abstract forms into ideas that suddenly made sense.

"Think" didn't move me to think. It did even better. I experienced a complete and immediate rush, as if endorphins had been injected directly into my bloodstream. Had I been a teenager, I would have shrieked gleefully, stomped my feet, jumped up and down on my seat. I did none of the above—but I became hooked on a sensation that my brain's reward system, from that moment forward, would seek to reproduce as often as it could.

Having fun.

I smile secretly, just thinking about it.

Vicky Tiel, fashion designer

· ·

I WAS IN fashion school at Parsons. I had this fabulous apartment in Greenwich Village on Jones Street between West Fourth and Bleecker. All the girls in school stayed in dorms and had to live in shared apartments but, thanks to my father, who was a builder in Washington and was very successful, I had a floor-through in a brownstone with two working fireplaces and a brick wall all along one side.

I had created a business, selling dresses in my apartment for cash. I had hung the clothes on nails in the brick wall; there must have been twenty items there. I concentrated on leather, which I thought was a really good thing. I sold leather coats and miniskirts—they were the first minis ever—and suede bags. I fringed them all and worked beads into the fringe. I had fringed vests and skirts.

The Cafe Wha? down the street was the center of life at that time. Dylan performed there, although he was known as Bobby Zimmerman then. But he wasn't the number one singer at the Wha?—that was Steve DeNaut, who was then my boyfriend. Steve didn't sing hillbilly music or soul music but a combination of everything else. His music, like that of Dave Van Ronk and Dylan, was folk, bluesy, country all mixed together. I'd say Woody Guthrie was the biggest influence. Nobody had anything new.

One night in October or November 1963 Steve came to my apartment, put a 45 [rpm record] on the record player, and said, "Listen to this, baby." He set "She Loves You" to repeat on the record player. Steve and I started to make love. At the point where it changes beats he stopped in the middle of having sex. "Listen to this!" he said. The music went down to another beat. He said "Nobody fucking *does* that! That's *no!* And the 'yeah yeah yeah'? That's fucking *no!* Nobody *does* that!"

I asked him what he meant and he said, "It's a new type of music. I've never heard anything like it. And it's fantastic." And then he added: "I'm finished. It's over. It's over for all of us." (It wasn't long before he left town and became an actor in California instead.)

AFTER THE BEATLES came over and that time with Steve, I went to Paris. It was the spring of 1964, and I took miniskirts I created with Mia [Fonssagrives, who became the other half of the fashion label Fonssagrives-Tiel], [the photographer] Irving Penn's stepdaughter. Mia and I ended up getting photographed all the time and we made the front page of the *International Herald Tribune* and then we made *Life* magazine—I had five pages in *Life*. We were in the London *Times*.

We got hired by [the British chain] Wallis Shops to make clothes and I met the Beatles at a party given by Victor Lownes. Lownes was the owner of the Playboy Club, which was in a five-story building near the Dorchester Hotel. He owned a town house in London—the whole building—and every Saturday night all of London went to his parties. I had just graduated from fashion school and I met the Beatles there. Ringo's wife, Maureen, liked what I was wearing and I immediately made some minidresses for her. I didn't know Ringo then, I just knew Maureen. I dressed her for two or three years.

I had started the minidress. Then Mia made a wrap skirt which she wore with a vest. We made a wrap dress for a 1967 movie called *Candy*, which starred Ringo. He takes the dress off Candy in the movie—that's how I got to know Ringo. By the time we did the movie he had divorced Maureen and married a very famous model, Barbara Bach, a beautiful girl.

I created the costumes for that movie in 1965. Ringo was busy unwrapping the star of *Candy* three years before Diane Von Furstenberg "invented" the wrap dress! Fashion is such BS, you know?

Tom Long, fan

· ·

My memory of the Beatles' splash was at St. James elementary school in Syracuse, New York. A classmate, Leon Shattel, brought in his older sister's records to play in our fourth-grade classroom.

St. James was staffed by Franciscan nuns who were generally older, dour women who weren't afraid to practice corporal punishment on students at any given moment. I was in my fifth year of parochial education by now and you had better have figured out what not to do to avoid being beat with a hardwood pointer.

Not all of the penguins were old. I recall a younger recruit that year who allowed these Beatles records, 45-rpm singles, to be played in class. The teacher would sing along almost hypnotically, as if an out of body experience was taking place.

This was all very interesting to observe. The message was mixed, at best. A nun, who was undoubtedly living a very austere existence dictated by older, possibly sadistic nuns, singing along to "I Want to Hold Your Hand."

I later made a career in rock and roll, as a soundman and roadie. I don't want to say that this moment set me on that path, but it could have been when that kind of music entered my life. Whatever it was, I filed it under one of my father's many classic quotes: "Life is *Mad* magazine."

Janis Ian, musician

. . . .

I DIDN'T GROW up on pop music, I grew up on classical and jazz and folk. The first time I ever paid any attention to a pop song was whenever the Beach Boys came out with "Little Deuce Coupe"—I couldn't believe how great the harmonies were.

Otherwise pop was really off my radar. When *A Hard Day's Night* came out in 1964 I was thirteen and attending summer camp with a bunch of other campers, including my friend Janey Street who was a *huge* Beatles and Stones fan. We took the camp truck into town, to the local movie theatre in Pawling or Poughkeepsie, New York, to see the film.

I came out of that film a convert. We sang Beatles songs all the way back to camp, singing them just as we would have sung folk songs, and we all started learning them next day on the guitar, and that was kind of it.

For me the Beatles were an introduction to a world of completely different energy than that of folk music or classical or jazz. The energy when Lennon and McCartney joined voices and harmonized and sang in unison was astonishing.

My favorite Beatle was George because I thought he was really adorable. But also because I thought he was the most musicianlike of the four, although in retrospect Ringo probably was, in a lot of ways. Still, George seemed like the one who was the hungriest to become a great player—and that's what I was interested in.

I was already writing songs by then. I wrote "Hair of Spun Gold" at twelve and "Society's Child" at fourteen. As I began writing songs, I began reaching out for a broader influence than what I'd grown up with, which was already pretty broad. Once I started writing for myself, I, like any artist, became a sponge.

THE BEATLES WERE fully formed by the time they started recording. From then on they just amplified what they were doing. If you listen to that first album, *Meet the Beatles*, it's incredible. It really shows how much time they spent on stage, working out arrangements.

They were on stage constantly, honing their performances and honing themselves. I think the impact of all that time on stage together is very clear, particularly in the first and second albums. There's a very different dynamic that happens to a song when you've played it live a lot in front of audiences. It's completely different from playing it in rehearsal or in your bedroom. The song itself morphs, and the arrangement morphs. Everything changes.

The Beatles have talked often enough in the press about how a lot of the time they were the only people they would see on a day-to-day basis other than their tour manager and manager. When you're in that kind of maelstrom, forced to spend a lot of time together but alone, you either get creative or you get stupid. They got creative.

Plus, they were *young*. It's a lot easier to move and to change when you're that young. We tend to forget that they were in their teens and early twenties when all of this happened. Their entire career arc as recording artists was all of seven years! I think in retrospect that they handled themselves remarkably well.

WHAT WAS IT about them musically? I think it was everything. It's that chord at the end of the intro to "A Hard Day's Night"—to put a 6th in there or a 7th add 13, I think it was?—in any case, it was an astonishing chord that you totally didn't expect. It may have been George Martin's chord, I don't know.

In a lot of the earlier Beatles albums the interesting chords smack either of Martin or of American pop music influences, as opposed to rock and roll ones. The fours and the suspended chords, the flatted nines, things like that, were not what you were used to hearing in pop. They also show what a great hand of a producer the Beatles had in George Martin. And wasn't Geoff Emerick the engineer on a lot of their record sessions? So, great engineering as well.

I DON'T THINK you can overestimate the Beatles' influence. They changed music forever, just as Dylan did. Nobody had done what they did—as writers, arrangers, singers—since jazz started and Bessie Smith had the first million seller.

The Beatles' impact was astonishing. And the fact that they accomplished everything in, what, seven years? It's unbelievable to have that kind of impact in that short a career span.

What a monumental influence they were on everybody!

I don't think we can discount the influence John Lennon had on poetry and stream of consciousness writing when he came out with *In His Own Write*. But then, you could argue that he was being just as influenced by the people he was being introduced to, such as Jack Kerouac and Allen Ginsberg. Bob Dylan's liner notes certainly influenced Lennon, as well.

So, it's hard to say where one shoe leaves off and the other one drops. . . .

A Way to Live in the World
by Carolyn See

· ·

MY HUSBAND AND I had just made a momentous move. We'd bought a house, but it was a house in name only—a cabin high in the wilds of Topanga Canyon, a firetrap settlement just north of L.A. No road led to the cabin, it stood at the top of a cliff. You climbed up a switchback path to get there, and there was a tram line, the kind Humphrey Bogart had in *The Treasure of the Sierra Madre*. In the daytime, sun filtered through the slats of the walls, and the place was infested with scorpions, tarantulas, black widow spiders, and the occasional snake. Our friends had helped to move us—we were still in graduate school and honorably poor—but most of them had gone home, leaving just one friend, a folklorist named Marina.

Have I said our friends thought we were insane? We sprawled on the couches that the lady who had lived there had left . . . because who could carry a couch down a cliff? We were filthy but couldn't bring ourselves to use the outdoor shower because of the black widows. Tom and I drank beer, along with Marina, and our little daughter Lisa sat, damp and pale and flaccid, as though she'd been drained of blood. We were exhausted but exuberant too, here at the top of a cliff where we couldn't get television; we were antsy, itchy, bored.

"We could drive down into Santa Monica and see the Beatles movie," Marina suggested.

As I remember it, Tom and I didn't even know who the Beatles were. Our heads were filled with notions of Milton's *Comus* and a thousand other unreadable things. We had just passed our qualifying oral exams. We were going to be PhDs in a couple of years. We had worked so hard! And now we were actually home "owners," even if our home was only twenty-three feet by twenty-three feet, with one downstairs room built entirely of orange crates.

But sure, we'd go to the movie. We needed a break, and Marina said the Beatles were wonderful. She seemed faintly scornful that we hadn't heard of them.

Now I come to a moment that changed my life. (And having written that, I had to get up and find a Kleenex to blow my nose and wipe my eyes.)

That chord! That chord that introduced *A Hard Day's Night*, along with the sight of those four boys running through the train station chased by hordes of girls, running, running until they found themselves in a train compartment with two older men. One of them was, well, "Who's that little old man?" "That's Paul's *grandfather*," one of them answered, and the grandfather snarled, baring his teeth. The other man—don't we all remember?—was some asshole English banker type and after some wrangling about whether the window should be closed or open John began to torment him from outside the train, running along, shouting, "Please, sir, can we have our ball back?" to inside the train where John snuggled up to his trainmate and said, "Give us a kiss."

All this in the first five minutes. Another way of looking at the world. "Give us a kiss." Give us a KISS?? Is that how you treat awful people?

We came home that night dazed with joy. Tom pulled out a shotgun and pulverized a couple of huge spiders and we slept outside that night under starry skies. We got up and went to work again, lighting the kerosene heater that heated up hot water for the shower and rolled up one or two of the five oriental rugs that the old lady had left, and at one point one of us asked the other two if he could have a hammer. "Hammuhs? No!" Marina said, and one of us said, "You filled his head with notions seemingly," and we went back to work.

But around seven one of us said, "Well, shall we?" and not even thinking about showers, we drove back down again into Santa Monica, to see *A Hard Day's Night*. During the following month we saw it twenty-three times, Marina went home and we still went to see it. We bought the Beatles' first album, which was divine, of course, but for me, in those days it was the world of the movie that held me in its arms.

George in the ad executive's office twanging a piece of modern art and remarking, to no one in particular, "You don't see too many of these around nowadays. . . ."

That ad exec fretting that George may have been "an early clue to the new direction," and then concluding, wrongly, that he's not.

Or John's playing with his toy submarine in the tub.

Or Paul's grandfather leering at a chesty broad and saying, "You must have been a great swimmer."

Or Poor Ringo, hounded by a waitress in a pub trying to foist off a sandwich as old as the hills, "that was fresh this morning!"

Or those moments when they escape, and one of them says, "We're out," and they spend ten minutes or so playing, just playing in the vacant lot outside.

WE HAD A lot of parties in the Topanga house that summer, even before the wall slats were repaired. One of the first guests, winded and cranky after his climb up the hill, took a look off our dilapidated balcony at the prickly landscape and opined that it looked like "The Garden of Eden after the atom bomb fell." He was right, the Canyon was a little dry. But as the seasons began to turn we saw its beauty unfold. Only a half hour away Southern California city life bustled; up in Topanga we could only see three houses down at the bottom of the cliff. One morning we saw a sweet young lady, stark naked, the sun catching the braces on her teeth glinting in the sun, doing a series of complex yoga poses. "You don't see too many of those nowadays," I said, and my husband answered, "Maybe it's an early clue to the new direction?"

Topanga was the delightful opposite to everything we had known before. Three enormous eucalyptus sheltered the cabin, a few cypress and clumps and clumps of California lilac, sumac it was called, and came in every shade of deep purple to sparkling white. There were webs and webs of an orange lacy thing called dodder, and the old lady who had lived here for years had put in beds of nasturtium and morning glory and for a few weeks every year the cliff was a carpet of orange and blue. We planted half a dozen citrus trees along the switchback path; they would grow up bushy, green and gold, brushing our arms as we trudged up the path carrying groceries, stamping the earth and chanting "Out of the way, snakes!" And for the most part they stayed out of the way. And we bought Beatles albums, and went to see *A Hard Day's Night*, all the while exploring what the movie told us, which was that there was a way to live in the world without working too hard, that there was a way to live in which we could play our days away. If we could only figure out how.

The story of *A Hard Day's Night* is simple. The day before a concert the boys catch a train ("Give us a kiss!") to a big city— all the while pursued by flocks of love-sick girls. They travel with three grown-ups; Paul's grandfather, he of the fiendish snarl, and two handlers, one of them Norm, who has hell's own amount of time opening a plastic milk carton, and his sidekick, whose name I don't remember. The function of the handlers is to keep the boys out of trouble and see that they don't have any fun. At their hotel that evening an invitation awaits them to a casino with a champagne buffet (which Paul, reading out loud, pronounces to rhyme with little Miss Muffet.) The grandfather barges into this posh event, leering at a lady with a huge chest, saying "You must have been a great swimmer." The boys make it out to a party, where a tall young man dances with such exuberance that he throws it all over and just begins dancing up and down. They've already been singing when they get a chance, Paul looking like the Virgin Mary herself, singing in the baggage car, but the next day begins in an everyday way with John in the bathtub playing with his submarines.

Their day begins with a publicity party where none of them can grab onto an hors d'oeuvre, and a lady journalist seductively asks Ringo, "Are you a Mod or a Rocker?" He thinks about it for a minute and replies, "I'm a mocker." And it's somewhere around in there that George wanders into the odious ad executive's office, twangs the modern art and tells the executive that the girl he's using as a selling lure is no more than a figure of fun: "We turn the sound down on her and say rude things. . . ."

By this time everyone we knew had a favorite Beatle. Paul, for those who preferred androgynous beauty; John, for those who prized intellect and wit; George, because he possessed that ineffable something we would later recognize as a spiritual life; and Ringo, patron saint of fuckups the world over. And everyone we knew had, by now, absorbed the message of the film: Have fun! Revere it—and of course, buy three Beatles albums.

Soon, a good part of our world began to smell strangely aromatic. Grass had invaded it. I remember my husband and I attending a party in the Hollywood Hills given for Brian Epstein, the Beatles' manager. He brought a house gift of pre-rolled, fat little joints and we were each given our own, instead of passing them around in the usual, civilized way. As a party it registered as Serene, with Oak Leaf clusters. We sat in a circle in straight chairs, our eyes closed, without a peep out of any of us. And inevitably (at least right-wing maniacs would say it was inevitable), LSD followed as night follows day. My first time my best friend stood watch over me, as I in turn watched flowers and marinated artichokes yawn and breathe, and George told me to relax and float downstream. This wasn't dying.

So our parties grew into the hundreds, with young adults spilling out and around our cliff, which was really just one side of an acoustical bowl which caught that sweet Beatles sound and amplified it out, sending it west to catch the waves of the Pacific, and south to twinkle over larger L.A.

My husband, when he took his first LSD, politely declined to have me as his watcher. "I might say something that would hurt your feelings," he said, not unkindly, "and neither one of us would like that." And my little sister, who had come to live with us the year before, took Timothy Leary's advice to "Turn on, tune in, drop out" a little too enthusiastically.

I remember one all-night party with wonderful food, wonderful music, and all the weed you could smoke, where Maureen grabbed a nice boy named Fast Eddie, crawled off underneath a sumac bush, and came in at dawn the next morning, sat on the dining room table kicking her heels, shaking off little grass buds that floated about her, oversized moats of light, catching the sun. She told me she had already done LSD a dozen times, injecting it into her foot, before she was eighteen. "I'm not the same person I was," she told me. And the Beatles albums became more and more complex. They were more beautiful than before, but—in my opinion at least—some of the raw joy was gone.

"The Beatles were the Christ child, all naive and like that," my husband told me. "The Stones are like the Devil. I like the Devil more, myself."

It was as if the world, having been given an overdose of joy, scratched it away like a pesky rash, leaving something inflamed and somehow infected beneath. If you could have anything you wanted, what would you choose? Love? Maybe not. Fun? I SAID, Maybe not!

Up north in San Francisco, people began to steal from the Free Store.

The last fourth of *A Hard Day's Night* takes a barely perceptive, melancholy tone. John, Paul, and George fall back on their own devices. The plot requires only that the Beatles show up for their performance later in the evening—so there's a fair amount of waiting going on. Ringo is left alone at the television station and finds himself in the commissary. He runs into Paul's grandfather, who berates him for reading a book.

"Books are good," Ringo says, and the grandfather leans in with his familiar snarl. "Paradin's better," he says, and suggests that since the other boys don't care for him, he'd be better off around and about, disconcerting pretty girls "with your cool appraisin' stare." Ringo buys it. He leaves the station, where various people begin to have a series of nervous breakdowns, including the producer, who grieves that if Ringo doesn't appear in time for the show, he, the producer, will end his career out in the sticks, doing "the news in Welsh."

But there's something funny going on with the show—that's already begun. No flower children, nothing remotely "new" or New Age-y—just a magician who works with pigeons, a piece from a Wagnerian opera, flocks of cheesy but madly traditional chorus girls. In other words, the same old thing. It took me maybe a dozen times of seeing this film to realize that the end was embedded in the story, inevitable and somewhat sad. Meanwhile, Ringo is out on the town. He buys a coat that doesn't fit him, lays his cloak down in front of a lovely woman like Sir Walter Raleigh did for Queen Elizabeth I, but the cloak covers a hole in the ground and the woman disappears. Finally, he encounters a little boy by the river and the two of them skip rocks for a while, while back at the station the boys go looking for him, and the executives, in an agony of warling around, shift into high gear. No songs in this part of the movie, just a tinkling tune of yearning and possible loss.

THE LAST PARTY we had at the old Topanga cabin was the wedding of my husband's best friend to his long-time girlfriend. It was at the height of the summer of love. A talented dressmaker ran up a dress for me that she'd made for Sharon Tate before she was impaled by members of the Manson Gang, and a long, green, beribboned shirt for my husband. "You're the flower, he's the stem," she enthused, but to tell the truth, he seemed crabbier than usual. No matter. About three hundred guests climbed the cliff and drifted out over the ridge. My dad, who'd turned out to be a great stoner, stationed himself in the kitchen, rolled an end- less succession of blunts, and handed them out into the party. My sister Maureen was there, dusted with leaves and twigs, laughing like mad, and it wasn't until about one in the morn- ing that I found out my husband had been sleeping with a lady named Lynda and had one of those spectacularly depressing mo- ments that (also) change your life forever.

More than adultery, my husband was addicted to sermons.

He loved delivering them at the top of his voice, only now the Stones were his Scripture. "You can't always get what you want!" Over and over. He developed endless variations on this, until I finally began to believe it. It's the easiest thing in the world to believe.

You could say things went back to normal. John once said that the sixties went from 1967 to 1972. Over, all too soon. Today, I can say my two beautiful daughters are middle-aged women who don't smoke, or even take a drink. That man who got married at the top of the cliff is dead, as is his old girlfriend, as is his first wife. And my husband too, such a hell-raiser, who had a butterfly appliquéd on his crotch, who used to say, "Mescaline is a great teacher," died relatively young. My beautiful little sister died very young indeed, from too many drugs.

That resonant chord, the one that opens *A Hard Day's Night*—and there are those four lovely boys running toward us—opened a glowing moment in our history. The further into the past it recedes, the more "quaint" it becomes. But it was not. It was intensely real. The ability to experience joy, and perhaps to hold on to it, is in our grasp, if we let it be.

In the last scenes, the Beatles get down to work, or play. Winsome Paul, witty John, thoughtful George, goofy Ringo. You can pick up a DVD, or download them on an electronic device, and have them with you now.

Up, Up, Up
by Lisa See

. . . .

ON AUGUST 23, 1964, my father and his girlfriend took me to see the Beatles at the Hollywood Bowl. I was nine years old, a graduate of third grade. I wore a jumper, a long-sleeved white blouse with an embroidered collar, and patent leather Mary Janes. I held my dad's hand as we walked up, up, up through an effervescent and animatedly delirious river of girls—who were only a couple of years older than I was, but old enough to make me feel like I was still a little kid—until we reached the very top of the Bowl. We sat in the second to the last row of seats. The Beatles were so far away that they looked like little toy soldiers no more than two inches high. I hated all the screaming. I mean, SCREAMING. We could barely hear the songs.

I was not a Beatles fan. At the time, the musical taste in my mother and stepfather's house ran to Little Richard, Ray Charles, Chuck Berry, Gary "U.S." Bonds, mariachis and cojuntos, and Pacific jazz. My dad, who lived in a bungalow in Venice, liked to listen to pop music on his transistor radio while he painted. He often sang or whistled along to the Dixie Cups' "Chapel of Love," Lesley Gore's "You Don't Own Me," and Dion's "The Wanderer." My aunt, who was thirteen or so, loved the Beach Boys—a local group—so I loved them too. As for the Beatles, I thought they were dopey. "I Want to Hold Your Hand"? Yuck! "She Loves You"? So girlie! But I guess my dad thought the concert would be a nice treat for me . . . or maybe his girlfriend, an ethnomusicologist, was doing research.

I don't recall the opening act(s). This morning, when I looked online to see if I could find out, people seem to have all kinds of guesses: Sonny and Cher? The Righteous Brothers? (Perhaps we were there to see the Righteous Brothers, because my dad loved them.) Back then, the Hollywood Bowl had a large reflecting pool in front of the stage. What I remember most about the concert—apart from covering my ears and feeling very superior—is that girls started jumping into the pool, either in a desperate attempt to reach the Beatles or from their hysteria. Security guards hauled the girls out of the water, and even from so far away they looked like half-drowned cats. Dripping wet, they still struggled and fought, arms stretched out, legs flailing, to touch their favorite Beatle. I couldn't imagine doing anything so dumb. All around us, girls cried, screamed, wiped their eyes, screamed, held their cheeks, screamed, held onto each other, and screamed some more. I couldn't imagine doing any of those things either. (But not many years later, when I was a teenager myself, I would scream, jump, and dance at Cream, Hendrix, and Stones concerts. No public sobbing, though.)

On YouTube, I found photographs, a few clips, as well as the entire recording of the concert. The Beatles came on at 9:30 and played for just thirty minutes before being whisked away. In the audio, you can hear John, Paul, and George tuning their guitars. They sing "All My Loving," "Twist and Shout," and "You Can't Do That." Between every song, they take deep synchronized bows. (I'm sorry, but they still look like total dweebs.) At one point, John says, "The next song we're going to sing is an oldie . . . from last year." Then the boys break into "She Loves You." Later, Paul encourages the girls in the audience to clap their hands, stamp their feet, and "make as much noise as you'd like 'cause it's not our place anyway." You can hear them go wild as he sings the opening bars to "Can't Buy Me Love." The Beatles must have been on the road for some time already, or perhaps their voices were strained from trying to sing above the cacophony of screams, but both John and Paul sound hoarse.

It's odd to look back at that time now. As a country, we were still so innocent, as folks like to say. It had only been nine months since John F. Kennedy was assassinated, and more terrible things were about to come, but in that moment the future still looked bright and promising. My mother and stepfather fulfilled the American Dream by buying a house in Topanga Canyon, and I was enrolled in fourth grade in a new school. Right around the corner was the release of *A Hard Day's Night*, which would "loom large in our family legend." (See my mom's piece earlier in this volume.)

When I was in fifth grade, a new boy joined our class and was assigned the seat next to mine. His dad was an artist, whose photo would be included on the cover of *Sgt. Pepper's Lonely Hearts Club Band* in 1967. That same summer, my stepfather would go to Haight-Ashbury and come home a very changed man, with armloads of very different music. Not long after, I would smoke pot for the first time with my grandfather and the rest of the family. I was twelve.

Today the Hollywood Bowl's reflecting pool has been replaced with exclusive box seats. My husband and I are fortunate to have one of those boxes. Eight summer nights a year, we invite friends to join us for concerts. I often tell people about my experience seeing the Beatles from the second to the last row. If they are of a certain age, they think it's cool. But if my son comes and brings a date, she looks at me as though I'm the oldest person on earth. Perhaps I am. *Yeah, yeah, yeah.*

Joann Marie Pugliese Flood, fan

(the girl on the far left in the photo)

I HEARD THEY were a sensation. It was near the end of '63.

"I Want to Hold Your Hand" was what we heard first. The music was upbeat. It was happy. There was something about it that just pulled you right in. There was something about the sound. It was very different and unique.

I went to my local record store in the Bronx. I said, "This group, the Beatles? I heard their album's coming out. I want you to hold one for me." When the store owner called to tell me the album was in, I was so excited I ran to the store. I don't think I'd ever seen a picture of them at that point. I was just so excited about hearing more of their music.

When I saw the cover of *Meet the Beatles* with their faces half-shadowed out and their hair so long I thought, "How different! How cute!" There was something adorable about each one of them. But when I looked at Paul McCartney, I thought, "Oh boy!" He was just so cute and sweet looking. His eyes were so dreamy. There was just something about those eyes and that face. From that moment on he won my heart.

Vickie and I had known each other since we were four or five years old. We became best friends and were really close. We were together all the time. Vickie was at the apartment of her aunt—we called her "Auntie"—in the same building as my parents. I knocked on the door and Vickie and her cousin answered. "Vickie, look! *Meet the Beatles*!" Now we were over the top. That's how it started, really. We're staring at the album like they'll come out and talk to us. We played it, and screamed, "They're great! They're great!" We just loved the sound.

I HAD A big, reel-to-reel Webcor tape recorder and I used it to tape *The Ed Sullivan Show*. Vickie came to my house and we sat side-by-side on the floor and screamed in unison as we watched. My father was holding his ears because we were so loud. I turned off all the lights in the room and started taking pictures with my Kodak Brownie from the TV screen. We were so excited when we saw how the photos came out.

My father was in construction. He was a bricklayer and most of his work was in Manhattan. One day, after working in the lobby of the Warwick Hotel, he came home and said, "Guess what? I saw your friends the Beatles at work today. I was working in the lobby when this elevator door opens up and four guys came walking through."

He said, "You know, they're all kind of homely looking, except that one you like. You know, Paul? He was kind of cute."

Vickie, me, and a few other friends from school started running around to different hotels and someone on the street stopped us and said he was selling Beatles' mementos. The owner of the Riviera Idlewild Hotel, which was opposite the JFK International Arrivals building, sold forks, dishes, and bath towels that he said had been used by the Beatles. Each item came with an affidavit from the manager saying that it had been used by the band when they stayed in his hotel. I bought a piece of towel with a photo of Paul McCartney attached. I think I paid a dollar for it.

I still have that and a lot of other Beatles memorabilia, including my concert ticket stubs. My uncle Jack worked for BOAC [British Overseas Airways Corporation, now British Airways]. They had a Beatles Bahamas Special after the band finished filming *Help!* in Nassau and were on their way back to London. My uncle gave me a BOAC Welcomes Aboard the Beatles, March 1965 menu from their flight. They served fresh Canadian salmon with mayonnaise.

WE WENT TO the concert in Forest Hills, Queens, New York, on August 28, 1964. Vickie's parents drove us. It was just crazy, pandemonium, with people screaming so loud you couldn't hear a thing. We couldn't wait to hear the Beatles. We didn't really want to hear those "other guys" first but then later my cousin, Linda Belfi, said "Oh, they weren't too bad." It turns out "they" were the Righteous Brothers.

The concert is like a blur. We were sitting pretty far away from the stage. I think the Beatles were helicoptered in. They only played for about forty-five minutes. (I also went to their concert at Shea Stadium the following year.)

Vickie, my cousin Linda, and I decided to go down to the city on September 20. We knew the Beatles were going to be at the Paramount Theatre giving a benefit concert that evening, so we decided to hang out. They were staying at the Delmonico Hotel and we thought somehow we might see them. We wanted to be part of the whole scene. I took pictures of the hotel and crowd.

Linda made the sign. She's the girl on the right who has on an "I Love George" button. Back then she lived in Monsey, New York, up in Rockland County. Her father dropped her off at my house in the Bronx. We were going to take the train into the city. She had the sign and we were just so excited. I think she'd made the sign at her house in Monsey.

When she showed me the sign I said, "Guess what?" She had spelled the band's name B E A T E S. I got some Magic Marker and I put a little *L* in. You can see in the photo that it's small.

When we got to the hotel, we stood behind the police barricade and set up the sign. The curtains would move. I remember a hand waving out of the window on the fourth or fifth floor and everyone screaming.

I definitely remember a guy walking by with a camera. He saw the sign and he saw us and said he wanted to take a picture. He said he was a photographer for . . . but we didn't hear him. "Are we going to be in the newspaper?" we asked. He said, "Yeah, you probably are. Look for it this week."

Vickie and I were buying the *New York Daily News* for weeks, and the *Post*, too, looking and looking but it never appeared. My father read both papers regularly and he checked them, too. We never knew it was the *New York Times*. Or that the photo would become somewhat iconic.

THE BEATLES WERE very nonintimidating. They were cute. I loved their voices, their harmonies, and their British accents. They were very sweet and I think that was part of their appeal to girls our age. It was about love. They were writing from their hearts, without pyrotechnics and costume changes, and that's what I loved. It was rock 'n' roll, just music from the heart.

Most of us were innocent. A lot of us girls were probably between thirteen and fifteen—that was probably the average age. We weren't sexually active, we didn't have boyfriends.

I wasn't a fantasy person who would fall in love with someone they didn't know. But there was just something about them. . . . I even remember guys at my school who were really taken by them. You had your favorite and whoever that was you had a love crush on him. You thought, "Maybe I'll get to meet him one day."

I know a lot of girls thought that if she could only meet her Beatle he'd fall in love with her and she'd get to marry him. He'd choose her out of, you know, 500 million other girls. I always thought that was a little farfetched. I was more of a realist.

Years later, when my daughter Kristin was sixteen, I took her to hear Paul McCartney when he played in Tempe, Arizona. When they came on stage she was in awe. She said, "This is the best concert I've ever been to." We stood up, both of us, and waved our arms back and forth and sang the songs at the top of our lungs. She later told me, "Mom, I loved watching your eyes light up and you were so very happy." It gave her a glimpse into my teen years. I loved being able to share that part of my life with her.

I THINK IT was in October 2007 that Vickie called and said, "You've got to get a copy of *Vogue* magazine, the August issue.

Call me back when you get it." I said, "Vickie, I haven't seen you in ten or fifteen years, you don't say 'Hi, how're you doing?' You just say to get *Vogue* magazine? This is crazy!"

She told me to call her before I opened it, but I looked anyway. I thought it must have something to do with the Beatles. I turned to the article and all of a sudden I saw that picture and I thought, "Oh my God, there we are!" Then I saw your name and realized you must be the girl who was in the middle with the reddish hair.

Honestly, when Vickie called me it came at a time in my life that my heart was so very broken. I was devastated. My daughter, Kristin, had cancer. It, along with the chemo, was ravishing her body. At that point I was so depressed.

I hadn't thought of the Beatles in a long time. . . . When I saw the *Vogue* article it pulled me up. It was a little bit of a positive kick. It kind of brought all that happiness back and that fun and that excitement. It really lifted my spirits.

I remember making a photocopy of the article and sending it to my daughter. I was so excited. I was trying to make her happy. I knew that the article and photo would do just that. She grew up with a mother who loved the Beatles. Every birthday I would play her the song "Birthday" by the Beatles, or sing it to her, and it became a tradition.

Kristin passed away a couple of months later, in January 2008, when she was thirty-four. She was my only child. After she had passed, I was back here and very depressed. I was so down and distraught, I can't even tell you.

Then my neighbor told me about a local Arizona group he

heard called Marmalade Skies that plays Beatles songs. They're not imitating the Beatles, they're a tribute band. I thought, "I have to find out more about this group!" I signed up for their e-mail notifications. Believe it or not, the first one I received had that photo of us in it! There we all were, screaming behind the sign.

I just fell in love with this band. They're really great musically and just really nice people—all seven of them. I got to know them over the past years and it brought back some fun and some joy and some happiness. They just love the Beatles and were influenced by them growing up. One of the band members told me, "This is the best music in the world. The magic is in the music."

I don't think of things as coincidences. I think of things as being spiritual and "God things." When Vickie called it was such an uplift. It was the same with Marmalade Skies. Every time I see or hear that group I'm fifteen again.

Into the Future
by Pico Iyer

. . . .

SUDDENLY, THERE WERE black insects being shown crawling over our (black-and-white) screen on the 7:00 p.m. news broadcast, and the rather droll, highly cultured newscaster was saying something about beetles taking over the world.

I was only seven years old then, and not much ever seemed to happen in grey and red-brick North Oxford. My parents and I tuned in, near-religiously, to watch Lucille Ball and Dick Van Dyke on our rickety little monochrome TV, and occasionally got even stronger whiffs of the exotic new culture of glamour across the ocean when Perry Mason or the Beverly Hillbillies paid a house call. America, largely known to us through images on big screens, was everything the academic, tradition-heavy environment around us was not: open, spacious, freed from history. Outside our damp little rooms we trudged in the footsteps of ghosts who had been walking the same narrow pathways for centuries; onscreen—in our imaginations—we were free to take flight.

We'd heard of Mods and Rockers then, of teddy boys and skinny boys in skinny suits and ties standing rather woodenly on "Top of the Pops," playing sweet melodies and fast guitars. But we hadn't yet heard of the Who or the Stones—not in backward-looking Oxford—and this newscast was telling us about those mop-haired boys we'd previously associated with wanting to hold our hands and loving us yeah, yeah, yeah. Every time I came back from the little hairdressers in the Turl, our cleaning lady, Miss Bennett, would say, "He looks like a right little Beatle, he does." We hadn't yet moved on to discussing which one.

In the years to come, after we made our own move to America, sixteen months later, my father would sit in his study in the dry hills, rattlesnakes and tarantulas sometimes visible in the brush outside, and explain to his wide-eyed (and often psychedelically altered) students about the cover of the *Sgt. Pepper* album and what sitar ragas really meant in our ancestral India. The Beatles, very soon, would make the anarchism and the transcendental states of being my father liked to talk about fashionable, even de rigueur.

But for the moment they were the path-breakers while we, in dripping, slow-moving, ancient England, where shops never opened on Sundays and horizons seemed cut short by the grey walls next door, were watching their ascent with a mingled pride and envy. These peppy, well-mannered boys from Liverpool, whom you could easily imagine introducing to your mother, were taking off; England, which drew so much of its cultural energy and freshness from America, was threatening to offer something potent in return.

The copies of *The Listener* piled up in my father's study. "The popular newspapers [carried] pictures of girls screaming their heads off at concerts," as J. M. Coetzee wrote of the same period, in his memory book, *Youth*. Soon the Swinging Sixties would come to London, and Twiggy and David Bailey and Alfie and the rest might all seem to be coproduced by the Beatles. But for now the Beeb [BBC], in its auntish way, was making jokes for entomologists, and pretending that a lower form of insect was somehow taking that renegade colony across the water hostage.

It would be years before I realized that the name was actually spelled with an *a* and in fact represented a subversion much deeper than the BBC could acknowledge. Britain was no longer trapped inside the past and was offering the New World something even newer, more radical and current. The day the Beatles landed in New York City was the day the United Kingdom could finally see that it wasn't just yesterday's power, on the decline, but part of what would form tomorrow's trans-Atlantic axis. They were flying into the future, really—our future—and the next thing we knew, Britain would be branding itself as the new America, freshly awake after twenty years of deepest postwar sleep.

Fran Lebowitz, nonfan

· ·

AT SOME POINT in my adult life, probably about fifteen years ago, I was at a dinner party in New York City and Paul McCartney was there. There was a piano in the house and I was sitting on the piano bench before dinner talking to people when Paul McCartney came and sat down and started to play the piano. I turned around and said to him, "Hey, I'm trying to talk here." He was quite stunned.

It did not stop him from playing the piano. Everyone else, of course, *wanted* him to play the piano.

That's the level of Beatles fan I am.

THE ARRIVAL OF the Beatles didn't affect me at all. It wasn't just the Beatles, it's all pop music. I'm probably the most unreceptive person to pop music that ever existed. The Beatles made very little impression on me.

In the long run, they must have influenced my life in some way because they were such an enormous cultural influence. I mean, I know probably a million Beatles songs because you can't *not* know a million Beatles songs. But at the time, they barely registered, although I do remember watching them on *Ed Sullivan*.

Soon after they appeared on the horizon a boy in my junior high school class in Morris Township, New Jersey, came to school with his hair combed down like theirs. Boys had fairly short hair then and he had just combed his bangs down. I thought, "What a ridiculous thing to do." I thought he was a fool, a clown. I was like thirteen years old, fourteen years old. I thought it was clownish to imitate someone else.

He was also, by the way, taken to the principal's office. The school forced him to comb his hair back. I remember his name but I'm not going to say it because of course there's never an end to when you can be sued in this country.

Girls were buying these Beatles magazines and they were divided into armed camps over which Beatle they liked the best. All those people seemed ridiculous to me. It just seemed foolish.

I'M NOT SAYING that the Beatles are bad or that they aren't good. It's just that I don't care that much. I never found them exciting the way I did find the Stones exciting. I never quite understood the kind of erotic excitement of the Beatles. They always seemed so soft.

When the Stones appeared, I much preferred them. I would not say I was a rabid Stones fan, either, but I definitely preferred the Stones to the Beatles when that became a dividing line. There was a kind of warfare between Stones fans and Beatles fans.

I wasn't even in that war. I would say, "I like the Stones much better," but I didn't really care. I have a friend who just says to me, "You're just not a fan, Fran." I don't understand why people follow sports teams, I just don't get this whole thing.

I was even at that young age, as I am now, kind of a floater. I had close friends but I was never in a clique. I would just float around. The upside of this, which I've found to be true my entire life, is that you don't have to ascribe to the rules of each little group. You can just drop in.

I MAY NOT have cared that much about the Beatles, but if someone asked who my favorite was I always said, "Oh, I like Ringo." I like drumming quite a bit. I've been a drumming fan for half of my lifetime. I've even drummed myself.

I liked the personality of Ringo Starr. I still do. He was not, of course, the favorite in my school among the girls. Paul McCartney was far and away the favorite. He was the cute Beatle. So it was probably just a contrarian position to choose Ringo Starr.

People forget how men looked at the time. They looked so different. Just the fact that Ringo wore rings. Men didn't wear jewelry of any sort. The fact that Ringo wore rings was more startling from a look point of view than any of the other Beatles. The only difference really was that they combed their hair that way. Their hair seemed long at the time, but then soon it became short. All the rock musicians had much longer hair, so the Beatles ended up with the shortest.

Those suits they wore, those tight suits with velvet collars? I remember a boy coming to some school event where boys had to wear suits wearing one of those jackets with a velvet collar like the Beatles wore. I remember thinking that he looked so cheesy.

I just couldn't believe that people would imitate other people, that's the main thing that struck me. I still feel that way. Of course, people do this. Even adults do this. I once asked a fashion editor, "Why do you publish these pictures of these clothes, I mean these dresses that cost $180,000—who can buy them?" And she answered, "Well, they're not going to buy them, they're going to imitate them."

We're talking about grown women, not twelve-year-old girls. They'll buy some cheaper version a dress so that they can look kind of like this movie star who's wearing this $180,000 one that she didn't pay for? I guess it's just human nature to do this.

I NEVER HAD money when I was a child. It never would have occurred to me to go to see the Beatles when they came to Shea Stadium. For one thing, it cost money. I never would have asked my parents for money for something like that.

I would certainly never have wasted money on a record, that's for sure. I don't remember even buying them, although I had a rich friend who did. I remember going to her house and listening to *Sgt. Pepper* one million times because everyone thought it was a work of genius, that it had ironical depths. But I also remember smoking hash at the time—I think drugs added a lot to people's perceptions of the music.

And parents didn't like it either, which added to its appeal, I'm sure. People forget what parents were like in that time. Parents didn't like the Beatles, but basically parents didn't like *us*. People forget that. Parents didn't like the Beatles and they didn't like the Stones. Basically they didn't like *us*.

The relationship between teenagers and their parents was not calm then. Our parents were mad at us all the time. I don't mean me individually, although mine were mad at me all the time, but even better children than me had their parents mad at them all the time.

Most kids didn't have any say in the way their domestic life was conducted. I certainly had zero and it didn't appear to me that most people had much more than I had.

If you were in the car, which we were all the time since I grew up in a small New Jersey town, the person in charge of the radio in the car was whichever parent was driving. I would always try to get them to change the station, but it was pretty futile.

My parents listened to a radio station called WNEW that played the music of their youth—Big Band music, Frank Sinatra. There was a show called *Make Believe Ballroom* they were always listening to and I was always trying to get them to change the station. Actually, the result is that I ended up liking that music quite a bit.

My mother liked the Beatles somewhat but she was always comparing any male pop star to Frank Sinatra. None of them measured up. I'd ask, "Mom, do you like this or that?" but it was always, you know, Frank, Frank . . .

My mother had a huge number of jazz 78s, which I much preferred—I prefer jazz to almost all forms of music. Nothing compares to it musically.

I PLAYED CELLO as a child, very poorly but enthusiastically. My childhood hero was Leonard Bernstein. I watched his Young People's Concerts all the time. And there were children in the audience. Someone once asked me, "Did you ever go to one?" I said, "What are you talking about?" I never even thought of it. Of course I saw the children there, they were real children, they weren't actors, but I never thought, "Who are those children? What kind of life do you have to have that you're there?" I just never thought about it.

I guess it would be the same thing with the Beatles, except that I wasn't as interested in them as I was in Leonard Bernstein.

I don't know who those children were. I mean, they were children whose parents could buy those tickets, if that's how you got them. In any case, they weren't me.

I don't think it was unusual, by the way, the way I felt as a child, which is that it's another world, it has nothing to do with you. I didn't think of everything in relation to me, the way people do now.

It's the same with divorce. No one got divorced when I was a child—except for Elizabeth Taylor. She was the designated divorcée for the country. There were all sorts of other people, some of them children, who went to the Young People's Concerts, who actually went there, but they had no more to do with me than Elizabeth Taylor had to do with my mother. My mother wasn't a movie star. She wasn't about to leave my father for Richard Burton. She probably *would* have left my father for Richard Burton, but she didn't have the chance.

It's the same thing with the Young People's Concerts. I wasn't even thinking I could be part of that world. These things didn't seem like they were related to me.

THE POPE CAME to America when I was a child. I don't remember which Pope it was—John, I think.

He had a mass at Yankee Stadium and all the Catholic schools in the country had a contest, an essay contest, and a certain number of children were chosen to go to Yankee Stadium to see the Pope and get communion from him. There were a lot of Catholic schools in the town I grew up in and a lot of Catholic kids on my street. They were praying and hoping to get this—one kid who I didn't know from one of the schools in the neighborhood actually went.

Which leads me to the Beatles.

Now that I'm grown up, I actually know people who were in the audience when the Beatles first appeared on *The Ed Sullivan Show*. They were there, people of around my age who lived in New York at the time and whose parents may have been involved in the entertainment business.

And that's who was in that audience at *The Ed Sullivan Show*—kids of men who worked for a TV station or some related industry. Sigourney Weaver, for example, was there because her father was the head of NBC.

For me, having a father who worked for a television station was the kind of life I didn't even know existed. That's how distant the Beatles seemed to me. Going to see them would have been like going to see the Pope.

Not that I was in the running to go to see the Pope.

I was very interested in him, though, I have to say.

I'm not putting the Beatles in the same class as the Pope, although many people did, including John Lennon, who once said the Beatles were more popular than Jesus.

Michael Laven, fan

· ·

IT WAS FEBRUARY 1964. I was sixteen and a patient at Massachusetts General Hospital in Boston. I had a small growth on one of my toes, actually on my third metatarsal, and it required surgery to take a piece of bone out of my hip and graft it into my toe. It was reasonably invasive, not life threatening or life altering, but invasive nevertheless.

I had a double room and one evening the center of the San Francisco Warriors—the basketball team that preceded the Golden Gate Warriors—moved in. His team had played the Celtics the night before.

He was Nate Thurmond—6'11", all-American, a top guy in the NBA. (He was actually second to Wilt Chamberlain at the time.) He had gotten a pulled scrotum—as a sixteen-year-old this impressed me very deeply—in the game and ended up in the bed next to me.

I was a boy from the suburbs and I didn't know from black people. Suddenly there I was with this huge black guy, one so tall that his feet were sticking out from the end of his bed.

It was the early sixties and I was still a relatively conservative high school student. A few years later I started moving around the city, discovered marijuana, joined marches to the

Arlington Street Church for draft card burnings, listened to the Dead and Coltrane and had my world opened up. But at that point I was still a kid and the Celtics and the Beach Boys were my life.

Anyway, Nate Thurmond's teammates came to visit him before their next game. I was lying on my back in bed when suddenly I was surrounded by all these mammoth people. You know, they were sports people, so they were nice guys. It was, "Are you okay, kid?" that kind of thing. So they're all seven feet tall and I'm lying in bed and there's Nate Thurmond with his pulled scrotum and that same evening is when the Beatles were on *Ed Sullivan*. Everyone knew of the Beatles by then. There was a TV in the room and I tuned in. The show came on. I remember the band came on and the girls were screaming and it was so thrilling. I just remember the thrill of sitting in a hospital bed with a seven-foot black guy in the next bed whose feet were sticking out.

This really *is* a Beatles story, OK?

To me, it's the juxtaposition. The Beatles came out with their exuberance and I'm lying in bed in Mass. General watching on a black and white with a famous basketball player in the bed next to me and the screaming girls in the background.

They must have started with "I Want to Hold Your Hand," maybe not, and in some ways they were so clean cut. And there was Ed Sullivan with his "shoe" [the way he pronounced *show*]. He had that pinched Ed Sullivan accent, like he really needed to run to the bathroom, he was holding it in.

I met Thurmond again years later. I was living in San Francisco and discovered that he owned a restaurant called Big Nate's BBQ in the South of Market area. I went to it a few times and had ribs from him. It was a just a basic, humble rib shack with pictures of him on the walls.

Nate worked behind the counter. I think it may be one of those sad sports stories, the story of a guy before the salaries got big, who played his heart out, probably got hurt.

When I met him years later at the shack, I told him the story of him being in the bed next to me but he's an old sports guy and I don't think he remembered.

So there it is—my memory of the moment the Beatles played on *The Ed Sullivan Show* is mixed up with this 6'11" all-pro basketball player and his team towering over me. The memory is crystal clear. It's like where were you when Kennedy was shot. It has the same level of clarity for me.

An E-mail

from Phillip Lopate

....

new anthology request   Inbox x

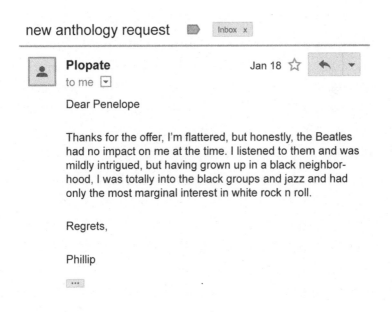

Plopate   Jan 18 ☆
to me ▾

Dear Penelope

Thanks for the offer, I'm flattered, but honestly, the Beatles
had no impact on me at the time. I listened to them and was
mildly intrigued, but having grown up in a black neighborhood, I was totally into the black groups and jazz and had
only the most marginal interest in white rock n roll.

Regrets,

Phillip

White Out
by Judy Juanita

....

AMERICAN SOCIETY WAS one big happy family in the 1950s. A melting pot, a Jell-O and white-bread land of perfection and gleaming surfaces. Not for a minute. The truth is, America was one big white out. Growing up in the fifties, my siblings and I had to choose between watching *Make Room for Daddy* or *I Love Lucy* for school-night television. On Sunday nights, though, the whole family watched *The Ed Sullivan Show* on our one set, the high point being when a performer of our race came on. (We didn't use the word *black* in self-description then.)

The famous colored pop artists—Sammy Davis Jr., Johnny Mathis, Leslie Uggams, Dionne Warwick, Nat King Cole— were so extraordinarily talented they seemed to glow. And yet they looked, to my adolescent eyes, like gifted pets of their benevolent white mentors (Frank Sinatra, Mitch Miller, Burt Bacharach), a status that befit the show's colorful menagerie of chimps, flamenco dancers, and sensations like Elvis Presley. Colored performers and musicians who seemed of independent mind—Harry Belafonte, Richie Havens, Odetta—had careers in folk or bluegrass, further from the mainstream.

The poet Amiri Baraka would say later the only good thing about television back then was that colored people weren't on it. There was a loss of dignity when black people entered the arena of television and had to do what white and white-minded directors and producers wanted them to do. Anyway, we weren't, for the most part, on TV at all, except for *Beulah* and a token on *Star Trek*. We were nowhere in advertising.

The sixties meant crew cuts, skinny ties, matching suits, "Teen Angel," the Beach Boys, the top forty playlist, 45-rpm records, spinning the songs. But in the parallel America, rhythm & blues (R&B) artists were busy providing the gritty backdrop to the violence and oppression of the American dream. Rioters, marchers, protesters, and regular folk followed a different drummer, doing as a popular 1964 song advised: getting "right down to the real nitty gritty." The breathlessness of the countdown to the top fifteen hits on "Your Hit Parade," sponsored by Lucky Strike cigarettes, matched the breathlessness of executions occurring with the same exciting regularity.

Nineteen sixty-three was a banner year for the black race. Things were heating up in the streets. That April, Martin Luther King wrote "Letter from Birmingham Jail" to white clergymen who wanted racial segregation to be addressed exclusively in courts, not the streets. The next month, Bull Connor set fire hoses and attack dogs on the marchers in Birmingham. August saw the March on Washington, timed to commemorate the Emancipation Proclamation's 100th anniversary—a great peak for the civil rights movement.

The miracle of television was a lucky strike for the civil rights movement. The abolitionist movement 100 years earlier had gained traction once the world, i.e. London society, understood the horror and treachery of slavery from ex-slaves like Frederick Douglass speaking abroad or from slave narratives. And similarly the civil rights movement gained universal spotlight once viewers saw the hosing, brutality, flaming buses, and overturned normalcy of a South under siege from protestors and arch segregationists.

The England–America exchange of influence went back and forth. At a Beatles concert in Plymouth, Great Britain, in November 1963, police used high-pressure hoses on screaming fans, a show of authority that matched the hosing of demonstrators in Birmingham six months earlier.

Meanwhile, there I was, a black girl in East Oakland, playing the string bass in my junior and senior high school orchestras. As we toured in school festivals throughout northern California, my fellow bassist, a member of the Escovedo musical family, tried to lure me into nightclubs for $10-a-night gigs. I knew better than to mention that to my strict Christian mother. But I loved music and craved it, especially Bo Diddley, Motown, and salsa. I often danced in front of my mirror for six hours at a clip.

Diddley had fused a 3-2 clave with rhythm and blues, and rock and roll. A Bo Diddley beat was a clave-based motif, clave being the name of the patterns played on two hardwood sticks in Afro-Cuban music ensembles. This syncopated accent on the "off beat" was perfect for the click-and-slip of my pelvis as I bopped around my bedroom dance floor in my early teens. I thought I had invented a new dance until I started partying

and found that this hip-click to the off beat was the way black
kids danced in the Bay Area. Thank goodness for osmosis.

In 1963 Sly Stone was a hip young DJ who hadn't yet
changed his birth name of Sylvester Stewart. He was fresh out
of Vallejo and the same CME/AME church gospel choir circuit I attended as a youth. He was firing up listeners in the San
Francisco Bay Area on KSOL which he nicknamed K-SOUL.
I had a painful crush on him.

My Oakland, pre-1964, was house parties, spiked punch,
segregated radio and five-channel TV, servicemen getting off
the ships at the Port of Oakland looking for a good time. My
Oakland, post-1964, was sets (nobody said house party, they
said, "Are you going to the set on Snake Rd.?"), marijuana,
stoned white college boys in khakis, hippies in VW buses
covered in psychedelic colors, Make Love Not War signs, and
longer hair on everybody. First came the swivel-hipped Elvis,
then Beatlemania, then the floodgates opened.

The Brits were shaking up American society once again.
When I first heard the Beatles, I got a pure musical thrill.
When I bumped into a black girl on the steps at my commu-
nity college listening as her plastic transistor radio played "I
Want to Hold Your Hand," her passion, all the more strange
because she was black, got my attention. Crushing on the
Beatles, she held on to a 45 of the song like it was a rare gem.

Being a black urban teen, I was into Motown, the Temptations, James Brown, Chuck Berry, the Supremes, and the
Moonglows. I didn't crush on the Beatles like I did with Sly,

Eddie Kendricks, and David Ruffin. But that's the good thing about it.

Of course, I didn't know what was happening technically, that on "Please Please Please" and "I Want to Hold Your Hand," the Beatles used a double back beat, i.e., an off beat played as a one-quarter note. But I knew something even better—I liked it and I could dance to it. The Beatles, a convergence of R&B and pop, brought a great swinging movement from blond to dark, from privileged surfer children in the suburbs to the darkness of Liverpool's working class, an amalgam that curiously celebrated its R&B roots.

Neither white nor black parents could control what happened after The Pill. By the time I watched the Beatles on *Ed Sullivan* in 1964 in my parents' living room, I had started college and knew a lot more about sex than I let on to my mother and father. All the prepubescent and adolescent white girls having orgasmic and orgiastic responses in public released a long-suppressed sexuality from its Victorian, Southern, and Puritan constraints. As these women let it rip in that prolonged moment of free public expression, I believe they freed up black women from whoredom, from bearing the brunt and hard edge of the white man's sexuality. We were no longer the only culturally sanctioned objects of naughty or forbidden sex, of plantation promiscuity. Stripping, nudity, free sex, skinny dipping, open marriage, group sex—sexuality came out of the closet and into the open.

Giddy with our post–high school hipness, my best friend and I regularly drove to San Francisco and hopped the cable car up to a nightclub called Copacabana West, where we danced with abandon all night. I didn't know about the connection to my black roots. Or that the United States embargo against Cuba cut off Americans from overt knowledge of the Cuban influence on music, especially R&B. I just loved being able to mambo, rumba, and cha-cha with a different partner for every spin on the floor. I loved the twenty- and thirty-minute sets.

Before the age of eighteen, we had been dying to get into Finnochio's, the all-male drag nightclub in North Beach that was like forbidden fruit. When finally we got past the velvet rope, the make-up looked caked, the wigs ratty, the clothing dirty, and the drag too uncool to be enjoyable, let alone believable. I was thoroughly disappointed.

In a sense, that was one more dismantling of the American sociocultural foundation underneath me. Just as Finnochio's female impersonators would give way to the Sisters of Perpetual Indulgence, as the gay pride, sexual freedom, and gender-equality movements strengthened, American media and television's near complete white out would be toppled by musical, cultural, and social protest.

Some look at the Beatles and say they appropriated black R&B, that they exploited it. But they acknowledged it as elemental and, by doing so, opened the door for Ike and Tina Turner, James Brown, and a host of performers—once colored, now black—to share some of the rewards. Touring abroad helped many acts from the chitlin circuit to beat the fabled seven-year lifespan of American pop music and extend their showbiz longevity abroad. (Getting their health to hold out and resisting drug abuse would prove as daunting a task as overcoming segregation.)

It's not too much to say the Beatles helped close the gap between colored and white America, the schism. Like a slap in the smug mug of white America, the Brits acknowledged black roots. They showed how white America had unapologetically ripped off black people for centuries, never giving a whole race credit for inventing the new American art forms of jazz, gospel, blues, and R&B. America never had been held accountable to blacks, morally, fiscally, or legally.

With the Beatles and the British invasion, black music and rock joined for a new backdrop to the morality play called American society. White wasn't completely out, but black was seeping in. The Beatles brought black music to the forefront. There it was on stage, front and center.

Renée Fleming, soprano

. . . .

My exposure to the Beatles began when I was in junior high school in Rochester, New York, and my English teacher did a unit on some of their songs. It was the first time anyone had ever suggested that lyrics or musicians, contemporary musicians in particular, could have a contribution to make to poetry or to culture in general. "Eleanor Rigby" was my favorite song in those days.

My next experience with them was in high school. I was in a small, select singing group and we did a Beatles medley. Later, I met my husband when I moved to New York, and I just heard the music all the time. He was a real Beatles fan, so I heard a lot of their music and learned a bit about it.

I've realized over time that very few songwriters have had such a longlasting influence as the Beatles. It's gone on for decades. Their popularity has been extraordinary, but their influence has been even more so. Their music is so stylistically broad, far-reaching, and of such an extraordinarily high quality that it has influenced not just the generation that came after them, but multiple generations of music lovers and songwriters.

Their music lends itself to many, many different treatments. Many of their songs, such as "In My Life" [which Fleming recorded in her 2005 album *Haunted Heart*], have been arranged in any number of combinations. They have a vivid timelessness to them.

Back when I was in college and singing jazz, I was mostly singing the American songbook, with just a few exceptions. I didn't sing the Beatles then. In those days, the repertoire was more specific. Now anything goes. People perform pretty much any piece they want, which is wonderful. There's more crossover.

As for singing "In My Life," well, the words are so poignant. The original version is so upbeat and heavily pop influenced. So when [pianist and composer, who played on *Haunted Heart*] Fred Hersch said, "Actually, let's look at the song this way," it gave it a completely different sound. I think it's beautiful and haunting and poignant. And the words already are.

What's interesting to me is that the Beatles were so young when they wrote that song and yet, for me, it's about imagining that you're at the end of your life and looking back. It's a statement about what's been most important. It's so interesting that they had the ability to do that!

I sang "In My Life" in the lower part of my voice, which is how I approach all popular music. It's more spoken. I don't have the ability to change how I produce my sound in my upper register. It takes a long time to develop the musculature and technique that we do for classical singing for singing without amplification, so when I listen to someone like Sutton Foster, or someone on Broadway who has a high belt, I think, "Boy, how do they do that?" but I wouldn't want to attempt to learn it at this point. I don't want to try to sing in a different way than I always have.

ANOTHER INTERESTING THING about the Beatles is that they became as well known as songwriters as they were as performers. Before that, from Elvis Presley to the crooners, people were performers and other people wrote the songs. There were so many wonderful generations of singers who sang beautiful tunes that were created by other people.

But the Beatles brought the songwriting front and center. It has such integrity and incredible variety. Each song is completely different—you would imagine that there was a whole team of songwriters at work creating music for the Beatles! Instead, it was this extraordinary gift of a couple of guys who happened to meet each other.

I love the quirkiness of some of the pieces, the level of experimentation. Even if it is a straightforward pop hook, there'll be something in the words that has more depth. And it goes both ways. Sometimes it's the music that's intriguing.

The music created by the Beatles has taken its place in the classical lexicon of popular music. It's going to continue to live, just as great classical music does. What makes it classic is that it stands the test of time. The Beatles' music will be around for a long time. It's going to go on and on.

Where Music Had to Go
by Anthony Scaduto

. . . .

"I HAD HEARD the Beatles in New York when they first hit," Dylan told me in 1971 as we sat in his studio. "Then, when we were driving through Colorado we had the radio on and eight of the ten top songs were Beatles songs. In Colorado! 'I Wanna Hold Your Hand,' all those early ones.

"They were doing things nobody was doing. Their chords were outrageous, just outrageous, and their harmonies made it all valid. You could only do that with other musicians. Even if you're playing your own chords you had to have other people playing with you. That was obvious. And it started me thinking about other people.

"But I just kept it to myself that I really dug them. Everybody else thought they were for the teenyboppers, that they were gonna pass right away. But it was obvious to me that they had staying power. I knew they were pointing the direction of where music had to go. I was not about to put up with other musicians, but in my head the Beatles were *it*. In Colorado, I started thinking it was so far out that I couldn't deal with it—eight in the Top Ten. It seemed to me a definite line was being drawn. This was something that never happened before.

It was outrageous, and I kept it in my mind. You see, there was a lot of hypocrisy all around, people saying it had to be either folk or rock. But I knew it didn't have to be like that. I dug what the Beatles were doing, and I always kept it in mind from back then."

Tom Rush, musician

. . . .

IN 1963, I was living in Cambridge, Massachusetts. I was a student at Harvard and I was spending way too much of my time hanging around local coffeehouses, such as the Unicorn and, in particular, one called the Club 47, which was in Harvard Square and kind of the flagship of the whole coffeehouse fleet.

Club 47 distinguished itself by being the place that went out and found the old-timers, the legends, and brought them to town. It was astounding. It was a tiny little place, an eighty-seat coffeehouse, but you could go in and sit at the feet of the Carter Family or bluesman Sleepy John Estes. You could listen to the legends yet also hear the local kids—Jim Kweskin's Jug Band, Geoff and Maria Muldaur, myself, and others including Joan Baez and Bob Dylan.

Dylan came through town a few times. I'm not sure he ever officially actually played at the club, but I know he was in there and he probably crawled onstage a couple of times. I don't know if he was booked as an act.

One of the things about Club 47 was that they took their purity very seriously. It was a strange, almost surreal thing because you had all these college kids sitting around singing about how tough it was on the chain gang and in the coal mines and all. But we figured that we could probably finesse this incongruity with enough sincerity, so we were *super* sincere. Still, there were those that really would get offended if you strayed—some of the same people who got so upset when Dylan went electric.

When I went electric, at about the same time, nobody seemed to notice. I guess they'd learned not to expect too much purity from me.

Most of my comrades-in-arms were specialists—some did nothing but delta blues, some sang Irish/Scottish ballads. There was a guy who did almost entirely Woody Guthrie songs. I was the generalist—I'd pick songs I liked from whatever genre. I didn't much care, as long as I loved the song. We were mostly focused on traditional folk material; there wasn't much songwriting going on—Dylan certainly led the way there. My first three albums, *Live at the Unicorn*, *Got a Mind to Ramble*, and *Blues, Songs and Ballads* (the first two done while I was still in college), consisted entirely of traditional songs. There was one, "Julie's Blues," that I "wrote" by mixing and matching existing blues lines—but that was the way most of the old blues were cobbled together.

There were all these conventions in the folk music scene, some of which were deliciously absurd. For example, you had to wear blue jeans and a work shirt to show that you were a rebel. I had a roommate at Harvard named Joe Boyd (who went on to produce Richard Thompson and Pink Floyd and the McGarrigle Sisters, on and on). When he was at school he was into blues and the folk stuff, but he also liked to wear a jacket and tie. So he was taken to task.

I remember some guy explaining to him, "You know, Joe, you don't have to wear a jacket and tie. You can wear whatever you want." He answered that what he wanted to wear, actually, was a jacket and tie. The other person was nonplussed, didn't know what to say. He finally told Joe that he *had* to wear a workshirt, "because that's what you wear when you can wear anything you want."

So there were all these incongruities.

THERE WAS THIS great outpouring of talent and energy in the late 1950s, with Chuck Berry and Elvis and the Everly Brothers and Fats Domino and others. One of the curious things about it was that none of these guys were remotely like each other. The Everly Brothers and Fats Domino were from different planets, but they were both big stars in the same time period.

And then it all went away quite abruptly.

For quite a while in the early 1960s there was nothing going on that appealed to us. We partly got into the folk music thing because what was on the radio was garbage. Folk music was a rebellion against it. Part of its appeal was that we really felt ownership. We may not have been working in the coal mines, but we'd found this music that wasn't on the radio. It was our private discovery.

Folk music goes back thousands of years. But for that one short period of time, traditional folk became pop music. But of course the pop Ferris wheel continually turns—whatever is in today is out tomorrow. So folk music became hugely popular and was the same thing as pop music for a little while, but then it shifted into folk rock and folk rock shifted into whatever came next. Then disco happened and it all stopped.

I LIKED THE Beatles' music right away. It was pretty undeniable. It kind of grabbed you. But it presented an existential dilemma for folk purists because you weren't supposed to like what was on the radio. There was an anti-pop-music subtext to the whole scene. When, for example, I played a Bo Diddley song, as I did occasionally, some people would get upset since he was considered to be a rock star.

So when the Beatles came along and all of a sudden there *was* something good on the radio, it was a bit disorienting at first. When they were first on the radio and their stuff was so compellingly wonderful, it initially presented a problem for some of us folksingers. Still, we embraced them pretty quickly. After all, they, too, were rebels. They had funny haircuts and were clearly doing things their own way. They weren't something that had been manufactured in the pop music factory. They were quickly accepted.

One of the bands in town, a mainstay of Club 47, was called the Charles River Valley Boys and they actually did an album, I think it was their second, called *Beatle Country,* in which they basically did bluegrass versions of a bunch of Beatles songs. (Albums were a big deal then—you couldn't make your own like you can now.) And then the Rolling Stones came hard on the

Beatles' heels and they also were very sexy and compelling and loud and raucous and rebellious.

One time I recorded a song called "If Your Man Gets Busted," which was a corruption of a Robert Johnson blues song called "If Your Man Gets Personal." I recorded it and Dylan loved it and he was carrying it around, playing it for everybody and he played it for the Beatles at some point.

He told me that he'd done it and I said, "Bob, what is it that you like about that particular track?" I mean, I liked it well enough but I didn't think it was head and shoulders above everything else. And he said, "Oh man, if you don't understand, you just don't understand." And that was about it. He never did tell me what the Beatles thought of it.

I bridle, at this point, at being called a folksinger. I don't think I am, because folk music is traditional songs and I do almost entirely composed material. Still, I play an acoustic guitar, so therefore I must be a folk singer. I've gotten tired of arguing about it.

Thawing Out
by Barbara Ehrenreich

. . . .

ROCK STRUCK WITH such force, in the 1950s and early 1960s, because the white world it entered was frozen over and brittle—not only physically immobilizing but emotionally restrained. In pre-rock middle-class teenage culture, for example, the requisite stance was *cool*, with the word connoting not just generic approval, as it does today, but a kind of aloofness, emotional affectlessness, and sense of superiority. Rock, with its demands for immediate and unguarded physical participation, thawed the coolness, summoned the body into action, and blasted the mind out of the isolation and guardedness that had come to define the Western personality.

Laura Tarrish, fan

. . . .

I WAS GIVEN three copies of *Meet the Beatles*, their first album, for my tenth birthday, in February 1964. From the moment I saw footage of the Beatles, I was officially and obsessively in love with Paul.

My father was very amused by my devotion. It was kind of a family affair. My mother let me order engraved stationery in the name of Mrs. Paul McCartney. On a business trip to L.A. my dad even went to Capitol Records just to see if he could get me Beatles posters, which he did. I'd make my father learn trivia about the Beatles and then grill him to make sure he was paying attention. I would interject unexpected questions into our conversations—"When is Paul's birthday?"—to test his memory. He seemed entertained by all of this.

For Christmas Dad bought me a share of stock in EMI [the Beatles' UK record company] and for many years they sent me invitations to their stockholders' meeting. I had a stock certificate for one share worth $4.75 and I would receive dividend checks for 32 cents. I never cashed them. After a certain period of time, they would reissue the check for 28 cents, then 22 cents, etc. I must have cost the company a fortune.

We lived in Phoenix and on Saturday mornings I'd go to

the library with my best friend and we'd do research on the Beatles. If they were going to be in a show, I'd cut out the listing. We wrote to magazines that featured articles on them and I wrote to Jane Asher [Paul's girlfriend] and asked her for a photograph, telling her I was doing a report on English actresses! She sent us a signed photo, which my friend and I then had to share.

I had a pen pal in England and we'd send each other news about the band. One letter very earnestly told me that she was sending me a surprise but was not at liberty to tell me how she got it. An autographed photo of the Beatles arrived soon after. In my fervor for the group, I chose to believe it was authentic.

I saved the covers to their albums. You'd hold the covers while you listened to the Beatles and read the liner notes. I have a Beatles collection somewhere in the basement. I even have the "butcher" one of *Introducing the Beatles* that has become a collector's item, which I got by steaming off the other cover. [The controversial original cover to this album (of the Beatles dressed as butchers and sitting amid decapitated baby dolls and chunks of meat) was covered by a more innocuous one before being replaced altogether.]

I snuck an eight-track tape recorder into the theater when *A Hard Day's Night* came out and to this day can recite most lines from the movie. I kept those tapes, too. Nothing takes me back to that time in my life more than watching *A Hard Day's Night*. It fills me with such joy when I see it or see snippets of it. It was such an innocent time.

For all my adoration and fervor, I never got to see them.

They never came to Phoenix. That was one of the reasons I was so mad at my parents for moving me away from Los Angeles when I was two and a half.

Years later, I lived in London for a time with my husband and children. Our flat looked out onto the Abbey Road crosswalk and we were just around the corner from Paul McCartney's house in St. John's Wood. We were there when George Harrison died and my then eight-year-old daughter (already a Beatles fan herself) went to the front of the Abbey Road Studios and joined in the masses writing messages on the wall.

As one of the youngest fans out there that day, she was interviewed by the BBC, telling them that she'd "grown up" with Beatles music and that George was her favorite Beatle. I was as touched by her devotion as my father had been by mine.

Screening the Beatles
by David Thomson

. . . .

IT WAS ALL happening so fast in a world that still moved slowly. "Love Me Do" went on sale in Britain in late 1962. "Please Please Me" was released in January 1963. In July 1962, Telstar, a communications satellite, had brought the first live instantaneous exchange between Britain and America—look at them, there they are! In 1963, in Britain, the Beatles did their first tour and the crowd went mad. The thing called "Beatlemania" was born. An American on vacation in Britain was there to witness it. His name was Ed Sullivan. He went to the boys' manager, Brian Epstein, and he said he had to have them on his show. Shazam!

ON APRIL 23, 1964, when I got home from work at Penguin Books in west London, my wife, Anne, had a story to tell. She had been walking our daughter Kate in a stroller over the railway bridge on the way to go shopping in Hounslow. It was an overcast morning—it still is, in the movie. Anne had seen what looked like a film being shot in the fields to her right. They were the Thornbury playing fields, in Isleworth, full of soccer at the weekends, but empty that day, except for what looked like a movie, with a crane and quite a lot of people. "Wonder what that was?" we said. We didn't have long to wait. By July 6, the film had opened and a few days later we saw it, *A Hard Day's Night*, and Anne could say, "That's what that was." Some people said it was the best bit of the film: "Can't Buy Me Love," with the boys running wild in the fields to that triumphant song.

Everyone knew the Beatles had to do a movie—look at Elvis, he had become a factory for bad movies that nearly crushed his vitality. (The best thing in any Elvis picture could be Ann-Margret dancing in *Viva Las Vegas*.) But no one had any idea how to do a Beatles movie. Amazingly, the project was a sidebar. The album for the film was reckoned to be far more lucrative. The film itself would be shot in seven weeks for about $500,000—in black and white! (To date, its rentals are over $6 million.)

The American company, United Artists, had thought of the movie in October 1963, just from the reports coming out of Britain. The boys took the deal but they were edgy about what the movie might be. "We didn't want to make a fuckin' shitty pop movie," said John. United Artists assigned Walter Shenson as the producer, Richard Lester would direct, and Alun Owen was hired to do a script. The first two were Americans, with not much experience. Owen was the key guy: he was Welsh, but he'd been raised in Liverpool, and he'd written a television play, *No Trams to Lime Street*, which some of the Beatles had seen and enjoyed. Moreover, Lester had worked with Owen on another TV show and they'd got on. Owen knew Liverpool language, so he hung out with the Beatles, listening to the way they talked. The important thing, he felt, was to get their cheeky, snarky talk, the way any gang sounded—with much more familiarity than respect, needling, teasing, wisecracking, with the amazement of realizing that they were *the Beatles* and everyone wanted them.

One reason why they had become a sensation in Britain was their chatty answering back, their irreverence and their mild insolence—taking the mickey, Brits called it, out of all the people from the media who wanted to interview them. Of course, mainly it was the songs that drove the enterprise, and the panache of the boys.

Looking back now, it's hard to miss the gay quality in the band. We know they were very heterosexual in life, but as a performing unit they were clean, tidy, and pals. They were a group, whereas Elvis and Jagger were full of sexual longing and aloneness. The Beatles had so little interest in or need for movie acting, and they would be shadows of themselves as individual performers. Their identity was as a group.

Their characters had impacted. They'd grown together, like a gang—but a nonthreatening one. Their manager, Brian Epstein, and producer, George Martin, had enough commercial sense not to frighten mothers. So when the girls howled, their moms could say, "Oh, that Paul and George—they're nice boys. And Ringo's fun." Of course, John wasn't like the rest, with his cutthroat voice. He was itching to make that clear.

Britain was a very different country in 1963 than what it is now, and pop singers were still well behaved and polite, like Cliff Richard and Adam Faith. But the Liverpool-Hamburg group offered so much more: true class hostility; generational rebellion; North Country contempt for soft Londoners; knowing the music was about sex; and realizing that they were getting so famous they were liberated and confined at the same time.

Kids loved the Beatles because they identified an urge to fuck the system. *Fuck* was not said yet, of course, but it was there between the lines. Scriptwriter Alun Owen knew the film depended on catching that "fuck you" attitude with the boys, giving a sly wink so we wouldn't really be offended. John especially found his artistic character (he'd have winced at that phrase—until he met Yoko) in press conferences. But there was another model for this unexpected directness: It was John Kennedy talking to the press, making jokes and seeming as if he was alive *now* and was scanning the crowd for the likeliest girls.

As for the director Richard Lester (born in Philadelphia), he had been raised in television and commercials, but had made a surreal slapstick eleven-minute movie, *The Running, Jumping & Standing Still Film* (with Peter Sellers and Spike Milligan). In hindsight you can see how it was a prelude, or working title, for the "Can't Buy Me Love" sequence. Lester liked short shots and plenty of cuts, knockout visuals, and a musicalized shooting style.

The Beatles were fans of the *Running, Jumping* film. That was important because the world was falling in place to do just about anything they suggested. Owen and Lester were both of the moment, hip, cool and subversive. London and Britain were not quite "swinging" yet, but you could feel the energy building.

So Lester called for several cameras and told their operators to keep shooting, to gather up accidents, improvs, and things that were way outside conventionally made movies. That air of cinema verité owed something to the French New Wave, and especially to Jean-Luc Godard, which was altering notions about film narrative. In addition, *A Hard Day's Night* established the iconography of the mopheads being chased through the streets by crazed girls who just wanted a touch. The boys' lack of privacy, something significant in their eventual breakup, was there in that first film. It was a showcase for the lads and their songs, but it was about celebrity.

There was an immediate follow-up, *Help!* It had Lester still, but no Alun Owen. Instead there were two ill-matched writers: the playwright Charles Wood and the crime novelist Marc Behm. *Help!* also had more input from John and Paul, who were wondering whether they might act and talk like artists, instead of Scouse* rascals. The film was in color, had many exotic locations, and was three times as expensive as *A Hard Day's Night*. It was more stylized than the first film—or was it more arty? It did as much business as the original, but now London was swinging and sophisticated, and drugs were part of that momentum.

By the time of *Magical Mystery Tour*, the four boys had become directors (along with a veteran cameraman, Bernard

* Scouse = the accent and dialect associated with Liverpool and Merseyside.

Knowles). *Mystery Tour* was made for television and done in color, but in 1967 few homes in Britain had color yet. So the picture hardly found an audience and, in hindsight, seems overloaded with the sweet, vapid pretentiousness of Paul (who was the chief intelligence on the picture). *Yellow Submarine* was still to come, but that was the vision of a Canadian animator, George Dunning. The Beatles were losing interest in movies and faith in themselves.

So it's worth asking the question: Could any of the boys have done movies on their own? The only one who seemed to have anything like a dramatic personality—abrasive but vulnerable— was John. He might have begun to play characters that resembled himself, in the way Mick Jagger became the recluse rock star, Turner, in *Performance*, which is a real and startling movie. Soon enough, Jagger proved he was no actor, and in all likelihood John had too much money, too many drugs, too much adulation, and too much Yoko to summon the spirit and energy for a whole movie. But it's just possible that he could have played Harold Pinter or even Joe Orton material. He was the only one of the four with a sufficiently interesting and unresolved personality.

By the end of the sixties, the business plan (let alone the artistic resolve) in rock had broken down and the concert film was taking control. *Woodstock* was vital in that process (budget $600,000; gross $13 million); while *Gimme Shelter*, in the best and worst ways, was a rock movie as a public event, culminating in murder at the Altamont concert. To this day, on stage and on camera, Jagger is one of the most fascinating, androgynous performers in the movie musical. You can't think of Paul in the same light, and the 208-minute documentary on George Harrison, *Living in the Material World*, made by Martin Scorsese, is too much of a dull thing.

Nothing matches the sound of the Beatles in those first few years, with the jarring, harsh-sweet interplay of John and Paul, and the serene cascade of their songs. The real moment of *A Hard Day's Night* is the odd, accidental way it captured the Beatles' cinema verité brusqueness in interviews, presaging the downfall of many humbug clichés in British life. But if the movie is about its moment, the "now" experience, and profound problems with satisfaction, then Jagger on stage on screen is everything that Elvis and the moptops failed to be.

The Ed Sullivan Show was February 9, 1964—73 million viewers were reported. *A Hard Day's Night* opened in New York on August 11, 1964. By then, every possible Liverpool gang was being signed up and touring the States. Next year, Bob Rafelson and Bert Schneider were putting together the Monkees. No one could keep up, least of all John, Paul, George, and Ringo. *A Hard Day's Night* was not a "fuckin' shitty pop movie," but it was almost a new kind of musical to rival what Jacques Demy was doing in France with *The Umbrellas of Cherbourg* (it opened at Cannes in May 1964). But that was pretty and the Beatles were gritty. The influences flew in all directions, and the Dick Lester style would take root in American television in 1967 with the pilot of *Rowan & Martin's Laugh-In*. A couple of years into the success of that show and the Beatles broke up.

So that's what that was.

Gabriel Kahane,
composer and songwriter

· ·

MY FATHER, JEFFREY Kahane, is a concert pianist and con-
ductor, but he grew up very much entrenched in the pop music
of his era. My parents are too young to have truly been hippies, but they had older siblings. They wanted to emulate their
adored elders and, as such, were listening to the Beatles at a
relatively young age, when they were ten or eleven.

When I was growing up my father would practice a Mozart
concerto, then put on *Abbey Road* or *Sgt. Pepper*. The Beatles,
along with Paul Simon and Joni Mitchell, are the artists I grew
up with and from whom I soaked up notions of craftsmanship
in songwriting.

I got to know the Beatles more or less in reverse order of
their discography. I grew up listening to *Sgt. Pepper*, *Abbey
Road*, "the White Album"; everything before that came for me
much later. Although I didn't start writing songs until I was
in my early twenties, having grown up with that music had a
profound effect on how I understood the DNA of songs.

There is this alchemical, sort of ineffable thing in Lennon-
McCartney compositions: as much as they may have been
writing independently, the ten percent of influence that one

of them may have had on the other makes their collaboration greater than the sum of its parts.

A lot of today's pop music—even that branded as art rock, independent, or highbrow—has become extraordinarily lazy with respect to craftsmanship in songwriting. There's this peculiar double standard, particularly around lyrics. A lot of independent pop music being made is really satisfying on a musical level—it can be compositionally rich, sophisticated, and moving—but not so in its lyrics.

The craft of writing them has really fallen off.

I think of Paul McCartney as a true craftsman. Some may view him as a cheeseball English music hall songwriter, but there's such incredible craft in his lyric writing and in his work as a storyteller. John Lennon, too. His approach to lyric writing was probably more intuitive than McCartney's; nevertheless, many of his lyrics have a really satisfying shape and structure.

"She's Leaving Home" comes to mind because the harmonic notes are so beautifully controlled; there's this kind of Schubertian quality to it. It was a favorite of Leonard Bernstein's in his quest to draw a connection between the German lied tradition and Lennon-McCartney. There's a perfect economy between melody and harmony. The harmony is relatively simple and the way that it supports the melody is as perfect as a Schubert song.

I can't assess a song like "She's Leaving Home" critically with any kind of objectivity because I listened to it from such an early age. It's wrapped up in the sonic equivalent of Proust's madeleine; it's evocative of so much from another time period.

I think of that song as a prototype, or archetype, of a certain kind of story song. Certainly a lot of my work as a songwriter— in my pop music writing probably less than in [his musical] *February House*—has been story songs. The two albums I've released as a songwriter, *Gabriel Kahane* and *Where are the Arms?* largely include these, as opposed to songs that are abstract and imagistic.

THE BEATLES STARTED more or less as a cover band. They had a repertoire of hundreds of cover songs that they played during their years in Germany. Many of these were American pop songs. McCartney has spoken explicitly about having a sort of apprenticeship to that songbook, and the huge impact it had on how he wrote songs.

Whether you're painting, writing symphonic music, or doing any other art form, you learn initially by imitation. By soaking up that material, the Beatles set themselves up to create a catalog of songs that were in conversation with an earlier body of work. You can draw a connection from the Tin Pan Alley songwriting tradition right up to McCartney. There are instances when he can be kind of cloying, or simultaneously amusing and cloying; those are most often in the songs that relate to that earlier tradition. "When I'm Sixty-Four," for example, has its charms, but it feels like a pastiche of an earlier song, perhaps one by Jerome Kern, one of the more explicitly Hebraic 1930s New York songwriters, with their chromatic melodies. (It's a little too chromatic to be in the Richard Rodgers vein.) That clarinet obbligato drives the pastiche home even further.

I think the reason the Beatles are arguably the greatest band in history is that you can close read the songs harmonically or texturally, but they operate on so many levels at once. The vast majority of Beatles fans are nonmusicians; what makes the work so great is that the craftsmanship doesn't need to be recognized as such. It's satisfying because it's simultaneously very sophisticated, yet incredibly simple and emotionally direct— and those are qualities that I look for in music.

Vera, Chuck and Dave
by Roy Blount Jr.

. . . .

I WAS BORN at the same time, roughly, as the Beatles, so when they hit the U.S. I was too old for mass hysteria. In retrospect, that may seem a shame. But having done puberty in the American South in the prime of Little Richard, I was not quick to see the pressing need for Liverpudlian rhythm and blues. And I was busy: in graduate school, scraping up acquaintance with Old English as a hedge against future unemployment. Soon I would be married. And approaching parenthood. And (hi-ho!) fulfilling a military obligation, incurred before I had any reason to suspect there might be a war. *A Hard Day's Night* struck me as slaphappy—callow compared to, say, *Duck Soup*. Did I mention that the Beatles were my age? And way ahead of me careerwise. And having *much* more fun.

But you couldn't maintain asperity toward the Beatles for long. The night before my daughter was born, her mother and I were dancing at Arthur, the club named for what Ringo—in reply to an interviewer's earnest query—called his haircut. One thing the Beatles were, that so few rock gods have been, was droll.

If you want to know what's wrong with pop culture today, compare the Beatles' "When I'm Sixty-Four" to the current hit song "Young and Beautiful." The latter was composed for the soundtrack of Baz Luhrmann's largely appalling adaptation of *The Great Gatsby*. The singer, Lana Del Rey, projecting an amorphously supra-ironic persona, asks us, over and over, "Will you still love me when I'm no longer young and beautiful?" When all she has left is her "aching soul"? Yes, she assures us, over and over, we will still love her.

But I don't love her already. Even when I was her age, I wouldn't have loved her. When I was her age I found a great deal more poignance and human interest in the comical appeal, "Will you still need me, / Will you still feed me . . ."

A book can't afford to quote published song lyrics extensively, and at any rate those of "Young and Beautiful" would gum up my keyboard, so I invite you to check out their godawful poetry online. Then set beside them the excellent light verse of "When I'm Sixty-Four." *Pfft* goes "Young and Beautiful." It's like putting salt on a slug.

The music of "Young and Beautiful" is grandiosely goopy, all the better to glom together words that have no intrinsic rhythm or coherence: "Channeling angels in a new age, now/ Hot summer nights, rock and roll. . . ."

"When I'm Sixty-Four," on the other hand, is as clickety and ingenious as syncopated clockwork. Looking back on this song, of which he was the primary author, Sir Paul McCartney said, "I liked 'Indicate precisely what . . .' I like words that are exact, that you might find on a form. It's a nice phrase, it scans."

Yes. Does anybody but Paul and me even know what *scans* means anymore? Can you, for instance, enjoy regular meter's potential for fascination? Does regularity make you shudder? Look at the lyrics of "When I'm Sixty-Four" laid out sans music. Every line (with one semi-exception) begins and ends with a stressed syllable. In each verse, the first and fifth lines are the same meter (*bum* ba-ba *bum ba*, *bum* ba-ba *bum*), as are the second and sixth and ninth (*bum* ba *bum* ba *bum*), and the seventh and eighth (*bum* ba-ba *bum bum*). And in each case the third (*bum* ba *bum* ba *bum* ba *bum* ba *bum*) and fourth (*bum* ba *bum* ba *bum*) go off on their own little trip. Each of the first, fourth and (except in the first stanza) fifth lines is halved by a comma. There are six question marks in a song that is one long question.

Two of the three bridges both go metrically like this:

You'll . . . be . . . bum . . . bum . . . bum
And if ba *bum* ba *bum*
bum bum bum bum bum

These lines sing themselves, but even the ones with identical meter sing differently. The song's potential monotony is relieved not only by clarinets, tubular bells, and eerie vocal background harmonies, but also by the sense: the mix of chipper and wistful in "who could ask for more?" is related to but different from that, two verses later, in "yours forever more."

And then there's the other little bridge, about renting a cottage on the Isle of Wight.

bum ba *bum* ba *bum* ba *bum* ba *bum* ba
bum ba bum ba bum

The other two bridges slow the pace, pulling back from the jumpiness of the verses. In this unique bridge, those first two lines (or maybe they amount to one line with extra beats squeezed in) are propulsive. Then the third line, "If it's not too dear," taps the brake to set up the other slow-down bridge, about scrimping and saving and the grandkids. Call this song nostalgic foolery if you like, but if you listen you can hear a real couple of people (Paul's parents if his Mum had lived?) back and forth in it.

"Rooty-tooty" is how Paul described "When I'm Sixty-Four." He was a teenager when he wrote it, on his father's piano, after his mother died. Juvenilia about old age sounds iffy, and many years after the boys bunged this quaint-seeming number into *Sgt. Pepper's Lonely Hearts Club Band*, Paul called it "very tongue-in-cheek and that to me is the attraction of it." But I don't find this song condescending, and I am seventy-two.

In his own maturity, Paul has stressed—excessively, in my view—that the song is a goof: "I mean, imagine having three kids called Vera, Chuck and Dave."

Well. You might say no one formal enough to name a child Vera would name another one Chuck—but these are grand-kids, might have different parents. Sir Paul at sixty-four had three grandchildren: Arthur (not named, I assume, for Ringo's hair), Elliott, and Miller. Pretty uniform, that string, but try working it into a song. Whereas "Vera, Chuck and Dave" can hold its own, for memorability, with any of these:

Tom, Dick, and Harry

Tinker to Evers to Chance

Matthew, Mark, Luke, and John

Manny, Moe, and Jack

Wynken, Blynken, and Nod

Hart, Schaffner & Marx

Crosby, Stills, Nash, and Young

Merrill Lynch, Pierce, Fenner, and Beane

Huey, Dewey, and Louie

Emerson, Lake & Palmer

Shadrach, Meshach, Abednego

Flopsy, Mopsy, and Cottontail

Hungerdunger, Hungerdunger, Hungerdunger, Hungerdunger, and McCormick

Hines, Hines, and Dad

The eldest, Vera, veracious but severe, probably overbears
the bouncy Chuck, when the three of them get together; but
plain cheerful Dave steps in to mediate. That's my sense of the
Fab Three. You may have your own. But surely we can agree
about how niftily the three names move in sequence: Veee-ra
[just a bit of a pause between beats, for the comma] Chook and
[two *ds* together] Dave.

Some commentators have assumed that Paul's original version was just the tune, to which John supplied the words, but
Lennon's own recollection was, "We just wrote a few more
words on it, like 'grandchildren on your knee,' and stuck in
'Vera, Chuck and Dave.'" *We*, you notice. I like to think John
tossed in "Vera," Paul added "Chuck," and Ringo, after a moment: "Dave."

John might have thought of Vera Lynn, whose songs ("We'll Meet Again" for instance) bolstered Britons during World War II. Or, being John, he might have flashed on Vera the hitchhiker in the movie *Detour*, one of the meanest dames in film noir. (The three principal characters in *Detour* are Vera, Charles Jr., and Al.) Conceivably he knew of Vladimir Nabokov's selflessly collaborative wife, Vera. Who knows? I named an elephant Vera once, for the movie whose screenplay I wrote, *Larger Than Life*. All I can say is, Vera seemed a good name for an elephant.

Frank Sinatra, we are told, loved "When I'm Sixty-Four" and called Paul to ask for something like it. Paul dredged up another little ditty from his teens, about a woman who lets men dominate her, called "Suicide." Sinatra hated it. "He thought I was having a go," Paul reminisced years later. "He was like, 'Is this guy for real?'"

Mysticism and psychedelics aside, the Beatles had many a go, all right, but they were for real. I knew it as soon as I heard "Vera, Chuck and Dave."

Linda Belfi Bartel, fan

(the girl on the far right in the photo)

WHAT CAPTURED ALL of my memories of my youth is when the Beatles hit America.

I can still see their faces from when they appeared on *Ed Sullivan* for the first time. I was either in eighth or ninth grade, sitting in front of our black-and-white TV, watching *The Ed Sullivan Show* and screaming and screaming so, you know, we couldn't hear them.

There was just something about them. They had such sweet faces. I remember the charming twinkle in Paul's eyes. I liked George, though. I knew all the women in the world wanted Paul. So in my own silly mind I figured I had a better chance getting George. That was the only reason. It was the stupidest thing, but that's why.

My parents were sitting in the living room with me. I think probably my brother walked out of the room at that point—we're five years apart, me being the oldest. My sister was there, too. She and I are eight years apart. She watched me acting like a nut, you know, sitting there and screaming to a television set.

I think of how patient my mother used to be, back when we had these old 45 records and played the songs over and over again. I'd listen while doing my homework; I just played and played and played them. I would not have the patience my parents did, listening to that music over and over and over, playing the same song or two. But they never one time complained.

You could buy these big, life-size posters of the Beatles back then. Everybody put them on their doors or on their walls, but not me! I had George Harrison on my ceiling, over my bed. My sister and I shared the room. What's so hysterical is that she tells me I would yell at her. She couldn't walk over to my side of the room and look up at the ceiling without me getting mad because I didn't want to share the Beatles with her. I'm surprised she still loves me.

ABOUT SIX MONTHS after they did *The Ed Sullivan Show,* the Beatles performed at Forest Hills Tennis Stadium. I remember that night like I was transported back in time. I met with my cousin, Joann [Flood]. She says we went there by train—I'll have to take her word about that. I remember sitting way, way up in the top of the stadium. It's mayhem. Everybody screaming, wanting the Beatles to come on stage. We're, like, "Come on!"

The Righteous Brothers opened for the Beatles. Everyone was booing them to get off the stage, including me. If you could have heard them booing! Then it dawned on us—these guys are really, really good. The stadium went from screaming and booing and "Get them off the stage" to "Man, you guys are really incredible" and really getting into their songs and their music. They sang "Unchained Melody." They soon became famous in their own right.

Then, finally, the moment comes, the Beatles come on stage. Thousands of girls at the top of their lungs, screaming. They probably heard us in Pennsylvania and New Jersey. The screaming! It was out of control. Absolutely. The girls were kind of swooning, including myself. I was screaming and screaming at the stage.

Then I remember thinking, "What are we screaming for? We came here to hear them but we can hear nobody but ourselves." I've always been the adventurous one. I started yelling at the girls around us, "Be quiet, we can't even hear them! We can't hear them sing!" I swear the stadium started taking on a different tone. It got a little bit quieter so we could actually hear their music. I remember that moment like I was there now.

And I remember the day of the sign. I made that big banner in the apartment in the Bronx where my cousin Joann lived. My parents must have driven me there from our home in Monsey, New York. I probably had the posterboard because my father, John Belfi, was a commercial artist. He was a famous cartoonist. I would have brought the pictures and lettering down to Joann's apartment with me.

I sat on the floor to make the poster. There was a long hallway when you came into her apartment. It was where Joann's brother and I always danced. We danced there to the Beatles and everything else. I made the poster there.

After I got it all together I noticed that, in my excitement, I didn't even spell Beatles right. My father was drawing cartoons for the *New York Times* and everything and I couldn't even spell "Beatles!" I had to go in and shove the *L* in there somehow. If you look at the picture, the *L* is a little higher than the rest.

ON THE DAY the Beatles came to town, the day the photo was taken, we got there early enough that we could stand toward the front of the crowd and hold the poster. We were there before their limousine arrived. When it pulled up, I broke through the police barricades. I ran underneath them and around the police horses and got to the limousine. I must have had a handkerchief with me—we didn't really use Kleenex back then—and I rubbed it all over the car.

Imagine, I turned out to be a senior vice president, but I was the little rule breaker when it came to an opportunity to get close to a star!

On the whole train ride back home, I was yelling at my cousin: "Don't touch my hand! Don't touch my hand! It's the hand that touched the Beatles' car!" And she was yelling back, telling me to shut up.

I don't remember the photograph being taken. We were so caught up in the excitement. So much happened. I only saw it many, many, many, many years afterward, when Joann sent it to me. I never knew it had been taken. It was, "Oh my God, look at that!" It was so amazing.

I don't think I ever got over my feeling for the Beatles, but the obsession itself probably ended when I graduated from high school.

YOU HAVE UPS and downs in your life. My first husband—I got married when I was nineteen—was killed in a car accident when I was twenty-three, after we had two kids. Many years later, at the very end of 1999, I moved to Texas to marry a Houstonian I met in Phoenix. He died five years afterward from cancer. I stayed. I've lived in Houston for thirteen years.

I've had a lot of sadness in my life with different deaths. I lost my baby granddaughter at birth just six months ago tomorrow. Shortly after that, my mother passed away.

It's not been easy, but I'm happy now. I'm engaged to a good man. I work for a community association company and really love what I do. I have three wonderful kids, two girls and one boy, and three grandchildren. They are joy.

ROCK AND ROLL was such a vital part of our lives. I don't think the newer, younger generations have the memory of the fantastic music that we had growing up. You learned the words really quickly and you sat there and sang along with them. To this day if you hear their music you still remember the words and you sing along to it.

I just love that era. When they have the oldies on the radio, say the Platters singing "In the Still of the Night," you know every single word. That's how it was with the Beatles. I could sing probably 90 percent of their songs and not miss a word. Their music touched your soul in places that no other group did.

The number one thing about music now is that I don't even understand what they're saying. They mumble. It's really sad. That said, if there's hip-hop on, I'll get up and dance to it.

Every time my cousin Joann and I talk, for some reason we go back to the Beatles. Whenever we talk about them, there's such a jolting connection between us. It's like it warps us back in time to when we were kids. Just a few months ago there was a Beatles special on and I called Joann and we were singing, watching it on TV, me in Texas and her in Arizona.

We take away memories that are special to us. That's what the Beatles did for me, created special, special memories. For Joann, too—her health has been really bad for most of her life. When we talk about these memories, she just gets giggling.

Instead of dwelling in negativity, you can replace it with happy memories, like being a teenager, sitting on the floor probably six inches away from *The Ed Sullivan Show* on the TV, screaming your bloody head off.

The era of the Beatles is so special. Just talking about them now, I'm like a little kid. I'm bippy-bopping around, dancing, getting goose bumps thinking about that time in my life.

Their music talked to you. It touched your soul and it made you joyous.

It still does.

David Dye,
radio show host

. . . .

I WAS IN Swarthmore Junior High School when the Beatles arrived in the U.S. Beatlemania was pretty universal. It was something that affected everybody. It was a cultural language that everybody spoke at the time.

With Philadelphia area kids, there were sort of two schools. There was the Motown school, the R&B school—these were people who were aware of the Beatles but who were not quite as into them as me and my friends.

I was into Motown but the Beatles had a special place.

The first 45 of theirs I bought was "I Want to Hold Your Hand" with "I Saw Her Standing There," on the flip side. What a great value! Two fabulous songs and I played it to death. I just remember how personally exciting it was to hear the harmonies and to hear these great songs.

I had the *Ed Sullivan* experience like everybody else. I remember my father watching with us and he'd say "Dave, the guy in the back, the drummer, that's the mother," because they all had long hair. It was like "Okay, Dad, thanks."

I loved everything Beatles and I saw the movies and I did all the things that everybody did.

My parents went to England and brought me back a British copy of *Revolver*. That album and *Rubber Soul* are at the heart of my love of the Beatles. They're the records that had the most profound effect on me. I really love folk rock and these records are as close as the Beatles came to that. Each one is just exquisite. They actually changed my taste in music.

THE BEATLES WERE still very present and very modern when I began at WMMR in Philadelphia in 1969. For me, becoming a disc jockey, they had a direct influence on my work.

In early progressive rock radio, you would blend records, putting them together in clever ways. The Beatles were doing this already on their albums. Starting with *Sgt. Pepper* and *Magical Mystery Tour*, they had a theatricality that other groups didn't. It came with that period of time.

These albums had that, as well as high production values. They inspired me in how to put sounds together. They made me want to figure out how to do it with other records.

In the early days of underground or progressive rock radio, you'd put together long strings of music. The idea was that the music would all relate to each other in one form or another. There would be some kind of connection, often a lyrical or a musical one.

A lot of it was done very extemporaneously. You'd just get in there and you'd do it. Sometimes you'd put a record on and you didn't know where you were going next.

When I played a song and was trying to think of what to follow it with, I could always find a Beatles song that would fit. There was always one that would work and that everybody would know. And there were a lot of them.

• • •

MY DAUGHTER IS now a junior in high school. She always surprises me. You can't play a Beatles song now—how many years later is this, forty, fifty?—that she doesn't know. I think, considering the changes that I've lived through in music, and what's popular now, to have that kind of cultural staying power is truly amazing.

I've interviewed Paul a couple of times. One of the things I asked him was how he manages to function as one of the most famous people on Earth. I asked if he could go out on the street and he said, yes, but the secret is to keep moving. "If I don't move, it's all over, these people are all around me, but if I keep moving it works out okay." I thought that was great.

I still use the Beatles a lot on World Café [his syndicated radio show]. I play them a lot and I love them.

The Back of the Album
by David Michaelis

. . . .

IN JUNE 1967, when I was nine, my brother and I were farmed out to summer camp in Vermont. In those days you went off with a fully packed trunk and spent more or less the whole summer far away from home. You were not allowed to bring anything that connected you with civilization, not even a transistor radio to follow the baseball season. But late one morning that July, I heard by chance the opening bars of a record that had somehow arrived in camp from the very epicenter of civilization. I had been on my contented way from archery, in the upper field, to woodworking, in the barn—a camp day that could just as easily have been taking place in 1947, because none of the traditional forms or craft lore of a boy's camp life had yet changed, as everything about the way we thought and dressed and did things was to change after 1967—when from the barn's shuttered hayloft the electric sound of *Sgt. Pepper's Lonely Hearts Club Band* bolted through the clean, sunny air.

The counselors' lounge was seedy and inaccessible, an outpost of adult mysteries. The physical presence of the new Beatles album up there behind closed doors created a charged atmosphere I will never forget. I was almost sick with the sheer nerve of it. I remember feeling pierced by the words—"It was twenty years ago today"—and in that first instant of listening in, the shock of the new Beatles record combined with the prestige of the counselor's lounge to produce an alternate reality.

Archery? Woodworking? I couldn't have cared less. Of course, I couldn't give them up either. I loved archery, I wanted to impress my parents with a Bowman's Medal, and as that summer went on—the Summer of Love, it turned out—I felt the clear, straight lines of my boyhood becoming blurred in a way I did not fully understand.

I knew a little about the Beatles already. I owned two Beatles records (*A Hard Day's Night* and *Beatles '65*), and when I was six and my brother seven, we had had Beatles wigs. They were oddly shaped, scruffy thatches of synthetic black hair. They fit over our heads like ladies' bathing caps and didn't look anything like the real thing. We didn't mind—these were *Beatles* wigs, and there was something insubordinate about wearing them, a kind of rampant disobedience that felt new and powerful. Years later, when I studied a passage of Milton that described Adam and Eve's childlike rebellion in Eden, I had a pang of joy and giddiness that reminded me of the sheer liberation I had felt each time I pushed my scalp through the hairy opening of my Beatles wig.

This new album was different, more complicated. This was no longer just a release of youthful energy; it was playful, as before, but there was now an elegiac tone in the words and music—and that was what made me feel I was entitled to the record's hidden truths. The previous summer, my parents had sat my brother and me down for an important talk. I knew before the word *separation* knifed into our living room that it really meant divorce. *Everything is going to be the same*, they said. *Nothing will change. We both love you very much.* It was my mother who for years afterward would say, *We're still a family.*

The message of *Sgt. Pepper* was that things were not as they seemed, which made me, I felt intuitively, the perfect student of its puzzles. Campers were not allowed to listen to records, much less the new Beatles album. But every day, it seemed, additional information about *Sgt. Pepper* came into circulation: a 20,000-Hz tone, audible only to dogs, had been recorded backward into the inner groove at the end of the British version of the album. It was said that dogs all over England were going bananas when tone arms on hi-fi sets failed to pick up automatically and instead drifted into the subversive inner groove of *Sgt. Pepper.* Every night, it seemed, the two counselors in my cabin discussed the album, quietly debating shades of meaning over our heads; I recall one of them telling the other that the reverberating piano chord (E major, held for forty-two seconds) gave him cold chills at the end of the record because it was *supposed* to make you think of a nuclear explosion.

It almost didn't matter that we couldn't hear the music, or the chiller chord that ended *A Day in the Life*, or the 20,000-Hz dog alarm. The mystification that surrounded the album had as much to do with the art on the record sleeve as it did with the record itself. Marijuana plants, for example, could be clearly seen in the photographic tableau on the *Sgt. Pepper* cover—*real pot plants*, daringly placed in plain sight at the Beatles' feet, or so the counselors said.

One night they brought the cover around for inspection. We each had a turn with it. The infamous tableau was as densely woven as a tapestry; it was hard to know where to look. Under the big blue Northern England sky, tiers of cutout faces, cloth figures, waxworks, ferns, potted palms, garden ornaments, and sculptural busts were arrayed around the flesh and blood Beatles, who, tiger bright in military-band regalia and holding brass and wind instruments instead of electric guitars, stood poker-faced behind a circusy Lonely Hearts Club Band drum skin. We tried to name faces in the crowd behind the band. Somebody pointed out Sonny Liston. There, too, was Marlon Brando from *The Wild One*, a popular poster image on the bedroom walls of older brothers in my neighborhood. I recognized the early Beatles as Madame Tussaud's wax figures, and I knew Bob Dylan—he was a folk singer. All else was unknown to me. I recall turning over the sleeve. There, vibrating in black print on a Chinese-red background, were the words.

It's hard to remember now what this meant then. To paraphrase Kenneth Tynan's remark about how *Citizen Kane* changed filmmaking, *Sgt. Pepper's Lonely Hearts Club Band* revolutionized pop music as the airplane revolutionized warfare. Until *Sgt. Pepper*, the pop single had dominated the recording industry, each 45-rpm record comprising two songs, the hit tune on side A, a lesser song on side B. Pop singles were marketed in a plain sleeve with minimal design elements and no sign that the lyrics were to be treated as anything more than bubble gum, chewed once and tossed away.

From *Introducing the Beatles* in 1963 to *Revolver* in 1966, the

Beatles had supplemented the traditional release of new hit singles with the annual appearances of two-sided LPs, the covers of
which, though increasingly brash and inventive, gave no warn-
ing of what *Sgt. Pepper* would unleash. Inside and out, everything about the record was narrative. It was bursting to tell a
story. On *Sgt. Pepper*, the Beatles made their regular instruments, from bass guitar to drums, sound like voices that had
something new to say, while making more conventional European instruments like the harpsichord and the fiddle, as well
as ancient instruments from Hindustani north Indian classical
music, seem integral to the most far-out aspirations of rock 'n'
roll. It was the first rock album to insert orchestral scoring for
narrative effects—one of many ways in which *Sgt. Pepper* was
created more in the manner of filmmaking than by the conventions of the recording industry. And if the recording processes
devised in the Abbey Road studios gave *Sgt. Pepper* the aura of
a mod film, the sumptuous packaging that the Beatles insisted
upon clothed the album in its most characteristic quality: read-
ability. Here was the first record ever to publish its lyrics on the
back of its sleeve. The songs told a story that was connected by
a theme and the story could be read cover to cover.

After that first eager glimpse of the album sleeve in camp, I
bought the record, with my mother, at Sam Goody's, on a visit
to Manhattan. Back in our living room, at the exact middle of
the sofa, where my mother's gay designer friend sat each of us
in turn to demonstrate the brand new effects of stereo (a scien-
tific moment that my father would previously have husbanded
us through), I settled into a habit of sitting cross-legged and

alone, ostentatiously studying the words on the back of *Sgt. Pepper* without playing the stereo at all. It was a deliberate act to *read* the Beatles without the music. Using eye instead of ear to ransack the lyrics for their hidden adult meanings turned even a ten-year-old into a seeker of ambiguity, an investigator of the imagination, a devotee of poetry. I had no musical ability then or now, and being given the words on a Chinese-red platter was like being rewarded in school with a period of free play. The literariness of Lennon and McCartney was just my speed. Looking-glass ties? Cellophane flowers that suddenly tower over your head and grow "so incredibly high"? A hole that needs fixing... Where had I heard this before? Of course: Alice on the riverbank, Alice down the Rabbit-Hole, Alice in the Garden of Live Flowers.

Sgt. Pepper seemed to be nothing less than an *Alice in Wonderland* for the brave new psychedelic world. Everything in Pepperland was reversed, just as in Lewis Carroll's mirror-crazy Wonderland. The Lonely Hearts Club Band was "in style" one moment, "out of style" the next. In "Getting Better," things got better because they could get no worse. In "Fixing a Hole," it really didn't matter "if I'm wrong—I'm right." Life in Pepperland flowed two ways at once: "within you and without you."

Curiouser and curiouser: the most forward-looking recording in the history of rock music began by looking back to a day twenty years in the past. Recorded tracks, when reversed and played back, had new and sometimes sexual meanings. ("Fuck me like a Superman," was one popular interpretation of the two-second track that plays after *A Day in the Life*; to me, it sounded more like "Never any other way.") The cover image was full of reversals: Old heroes were young again. Popular, beloved celebrities were "lonely hearts." The most globally renowned rock 'n' roll group had become the most parochial of municipal brass bands. Look in the flower-bed in the tableau's foreground, where the hottest name in 1960s show business— BEATLES—was spelled out in the most provincial form of display: municipal flower-bed lettering.

My true experience of *Sgt. Pepper* was as a reader. The word play, which I remember my mother's intellectual friends delighting in, was no more complicated than that which I had adored in Edward Lear's nonsense verse or in O. Henry's grifter stories, which had appeared in sixth-grade English. M. C. Escher, whose magic realism I encountered in math class, thanks to a brilliant and iconoclastic teacher, also showed that things were not as they seemed. The Beatles were asking the same question: *What's wrong with this picture?*

Over and over, I read the front and back of the album, from beginning to middle to end, trying to decode the tableau on the front and the strange, spangled words on the back.

The Beatles had written songs that set out to be *not* understandable. *Sgt. Pepper* was a world in which, instead of making clear-cut statements, you projected your own dream onto a cloud. It was like Zen: the song *was* the question. You had to go through a process of self-emptying before you could absorb the answer. But the album's organizing principle, its thought-outedness, took you . . . where? Back to itself. The Beatles coded their imagery, as all Romantic poets had, so that the younger generation, once it thought it had answered the riddle, could feel safe in its knowingness. *Sgt Pepper* belonged to a genre evergreen to adolescents: If you get it right, you will understand it, but the deeper truth is always one more magnification beyond where your nondreaming mind can see.

The Beatles gave you to understand, as James Joyce did, that you could spend the rest of your life making sense of what they were saying. If studying Beatles lyrics looked like a career in 1967, within a decade, an Ann Beattie story demonstrated how limited the duration of study had turned out to be. In Beattie's "A Vintage Thunderbird," the boorishness of a rival is characterized by the way he "complains tediously" that Paul McCartney had stolen words from the seventeenth-century English dramatist Thomas Dekker for "Golden Slumbers" on *Abbey Road*. If we can take Beattie's stories as true striations of literary archeology, then by 1977 the parsing of the Beatles songbook had become passé.

As a boy, I thought that the Beatles, like my parents, would last forever as the suave, avant-garde leaders of the culture. Whatever they wore in the early 1960s—go-go boots, mop haircuts, collarless jackets—everyone wore. By 1967, the Beatles, trapped by worldwide fame, weren't so much leaders of the culture as they were hostages to its molten center. *Sgt. Pepper* shows the Liverpool lads to be the voice of the age, the spokesmen for a cultural period that now seems as quaint and faraway as Dickens's London. The Beatles didn't invent the New, as I thought they did, so much as they invented an attitude through which to picture the New and the Old at the same

time. The costumes they chose for their *Sgt. Pepper* alter-egos
were takeoffs not just on the British imperial past but on the
swinging London of 1967, when kids flocked to Carnaby Street
and the King's Road to buy recycled police capes and brass-
buttoned military coats at boutiques with names like I Was
Lord Kitchener's Valet, which was also the title of a 1967 pop
song by the New Vaudeville Band ("Winchester Cathedral"
was their big single), whose chorus went:

Oh Lord Kitchener, what a to-do,
Everyone is wearing clothes that once belonged to you.
If you were alive today I'm sure you would explode,
If you took a stroll down the Portobello Road.

Rereading *Sgt. Pepper* more than thirty years later, I sat
down in my office in Washington, D.C., with the scuffed album from Sam Goody's—it's been marooned for years with
the rest of my records in a summer house where there's still a
record player. In my office, the only way to listen to music is on
a compact disc inserted into the Microsoft Windows Media
Player. I had not thought about it until now, but although I've
updated most of the music of my youth with CDs, *Sgt. Pepper*
is one of the albums that looks so ridiculous in the miniature
form (*Woodstock* is another: more than six square feet of visual
material shrunk to 4¾ by 5½ inches of plastic casing sealed by
the most infuriating packaging ever invented), I haven't had
the stomach to replace the original.

I scanned the back of the record sleeve where five newspaper-
column-size lines of unbelievably tiny black type still pulled

me right in with the opener: "It was twenty years ago today, Sgt. Pepper taught the band to play." I wanted to fall back right back into the audience—to "sit back and let the evening go." But the lines were hard to read, and not just because the record inside the sleeve had rubbed a white circle onto the printed surface, erasing entire words. The words are in memory anyway. I didn't need to read them in printed lines because they alighted automatically, almost too quickly, on my inner ear. It was as if I had written them myself, and therefore could no longer lay claim to what happens only once during the initial excitement of creation: an awakening to life itself. Coming from within, predigested and reconstituted, instead of fresh and new from without, the words had calcified.

What rereading without music did allow me to see, however, was how concrete a place Pepperland actually is, and how much the Beatles needed for their counterculture effects the solid institutions, the traditions, and even the architecture of the receding Empire—"all that Trafalgar Square stuff," as John Osborne, England's brash young playwright of the 1950s, referred to the country's crippling nostalgia. Hallowed British scenes and settings in "Lucy in the Sky with Diamonds"—"a boat on a river," "a bridge by a fountain," "a train in a station," a railway station "turnstile"—are blown apart and repatterned by "tangerine trees," "rocking horse people," "plasticene porters," a "girl with kaleidoscope eyes." Every bit of color-saturated 1967 psychedelia comes alive because of the contrast with images of drab, gray, post-war England.

At John Lennon's direction, the record's brilliant producer,

George Martin, created the swirly, Victorian, and very English effects in the sawdust circus world of "Being for the Benefit of Mr. Kite." Martin found recordings of old-fashioned steam organs, then scissored the tape into fifteen-inch segments, instructing Geoff Emerick, the recording engineer, to toss the lengths of tape into the air, pick them up, and re-splice the bits into a new whole. That kind of Dadaist approach, while emblematic of the experiments that made *Sgt. Pepper* a mirror image of its time, could only work musically within the formal structure that Lennon and McCartney and Martin actually felt most comfortable working in. The lyrics of "Mr. Kite" may have sounded far-out to the ear in 1967, but "a splendid time is guaranteed for all" and the rest were sentences transposed verbatim from an 1843 circus poster that John Lennon bought in an antique shop in Sevenoaks, Kent.

Throughout *Sgt. Pepper*, English place names (Bishopsgate; the Isle of Wight; Blackburn, Lancashire), British institutions (the old school; tea time; the House of Lords; the English army; the Royal Albert Hall) and English types (the grandchildren, Vera, Chuck, and Dave; Mr. Kite; the Hendersons; a man from the motor trade; Rita, a meter maid) are presented alternately as extensions of British greatness or as fading rays in the imperial sunset. The album's themes are anchored, more than I realized, in a period when England was looking back—part wistfully, part skeptically—to a world in which, more often than not, the "English army *had* just won the war," although the 1967 narrator of "A Day in the Life" can remember the Empire's glory only from seeing it in a movie. The "twenty years ago today" that seems to invite the audience of a brass band concert to look backward to an earlier, better time is actually pinpointing 1947 as the date from which the rest of the "show" follows—a year when Britain, lately in command of one fifth of the globe, was coming to terms with its weakened island. Awash in historical nostalgia for what had been, the English people could easily recognize the symbols in John Osborne's bitter play, *The Entertainer*, in which a collapsed music hall player says, "Don't clap too loud, it's a very old building," a reference less to anything architectural than to the decay of England itself.

The Beatles, grandchildren of Victorians, understood in their twenties that they were witnessing not just the end of English folk arts—such as the music hall variety show and the brass bands that had played leafy parks in every corner of the British Empire—but of something significant about the English character. Their lives had begun during the last crucial test of the British people. The births of Richard Starkey in July 1940 and John Lennon in October 1940 and Paul McCartney in June 1942 and George Harrison in February 1943 coincided with England's darkest but finest hours. Hitler's Blitzkrieg, the Nazi seizure of Paris, the fall of France, the collapse of the Chamberlain government, the rise of Winston Churchill, the Luftwaffe's bombing of England, and the Battle of Britain all took place in the five months before John Winston Lennon's mother and aunt gave him a middle name inspired by Churchillian greatness. Twenty-five years later, Sir Winston's death and state funeral in January 1965 marked the final

organizing moment of Britain's decline and the full flowering
of Victorian nostalgia.

By 1967, the Beatles, driving force of the New and the Now,
stood on the infamous cover of *Sgt. Pepper* like the gatekeepers
of history. They had learned from their brief lives as world celebrities that things were not always as they appeared to be. In
The Beatles Anthology, the millennial recounting of Beatles'
history by the lads themselves, Paul McCartney notes that
"what we were saying about history . . . [was that] all history
is a lie, because every fact that gets reported gets distorted."
Every kind of falsehood and misinterpretation had by then
been reported about the Beatles and their music; untruth had
freed them to create their own narrative, choose their own heroes, reinvent history.

Behind them on the album cover, in a collage meant to illus-
trate their sense of the precise present moment of 1967, stood
their handpicked representatives of the collective cultural past.
Into this pantheon, the Beatles elevated a host of American
movie stars and comedians, along with gurus and yogis, writers
and painters (though not many musicians), Liverpool soccer
heroes, and some seemingly conventional British figures whose
lives contained surprise twists, such as the writer Aldous Huxley,
whose experiments with LSD and mescaline in the early 1950s
had led him to coin the word *psychedelic*. Although the ficti-
tious military band leader Sergeant Pepper appeared only as a
handout that came with the album—on a square of cardboard
that also included bonus moustaches, badges, sergeant stripes,
and other paraphernalia—I was interested to learn that there

had been a real-life figure named Pepper: one of the many re-
tired army officers of the British Raj in India who used their
military ranks when playing for the local cricket team. Sergeant Pepper played for Uttar Pradesh.

Peering into the cover tableau now, I see, of course, that the
famous marijuana plants were nothing but greenery—a spiky
houseplant whose Latin name, *Peperomia*, was another inside
joke. I look at John, Ringo, Paul, and George, and see them
consciously distancing themselves from the viewer. The band
is photographed through a filter, with a deep-focus lens, and
there's an extreme, almost deathlike stillness on every surface.
After the fantastic energy of their first five years, the Beatles
are stepping back into the depths of time. They are reaching
into depths previously unexplored, pursuing mysteries, defining the present in terms of a magic past. The sense of mourning that fanatical fans sensed in the *Sgt. Pepper* cover tableau,
which they believed signified a concealed set of clues pointing
to the unannounced death of Paul McCartney, is, in a more
real sense, a eulogy to lost childhood. The four young men on
that record have no idea how, or even if, they are going to grow
up, and if they do, how they will ever stay together as a band.

Standing among the totems of their Liverpudlian Eden,
pantomiming the gestures of a dying Empire, the Beatles were
taking a first step out of their dizzyingly successful unadult
lives and looking back through the whirlpool of LSD to the
solid England of Lennon and McCartney's boyhood dreaming to invent the first, maybe the only, pure psychedelic rock
masterwork. For only through the quirk of having to market

in February 1967 a double-A-side single did Beatles producer George Martin omit from the album itself "Strawberry Fields Forever," Lennon's memory of a Salvation Army band playing an annual concert at Strawberry Field, the children's home near his own backyard, and "Penny Lane," McCartney's clean, sunlit paean to the English suburbs—a decision that Martin later regretted.

I had a similar feeling in a bookstore the other day, when I noticed that Paul McCartney had printed some of the *Sgt. Pepper* lyrics (among others from the Beatles songbook) in a spotlessly dust-jacketed volume of poetry—as if, in other words, they weren't songs and really *had* been poetry all long. I picked up the tidy white book and tried to read the familiar words in the state of aural blankness it demanded. But some right-brain part of me kept letting in the music. Great big windblown gusts of piccolo trumpets, percussion effects, and even a piano played through a Vox guitar amplifier with added reverb blew into Sir Paul's spotless white Parnassian tent, ruining his sherry party. It was an odd reaction: When I was a boy I read these lyrics on the back of the album as grail, whereas now, dressed up in white-tie, they seemed to have *lost* their poetry. Published formally, the words of *Sgt. Pepper* no longer looked excitingly Now; they looked very Then.

During earliest moody youth, most records entered my system for a while; I had a favorite song for various humors—an up song, a down song, a daydreaming song, a rebel song—and I memorized them all. After a season or two, those songs would pass out of me, and the record itself would remain external, a

fixed piece of a fixed time in the past, part of my increasingly
obsolete vinyl collection, an artifact of a lost age. *Sgt. Pepper*—
the name as an abstraction; the image I carry in memory of
its cover; even the original object itself, with the outline of
the record within visible as a rubbed white circle on the cardboard without—remains in and with me, like a plate connect-
ing halves of a broken bone. *Sgt. Pepper's Lonely Hearts Club
Band* had healing power, and in the summer of 1967, I needed
something I couldn't have found in the tourniquet instructions
in *The Boy Scout Handbook*. The Bowman's Medal I brought
home from camp, which I thought would somehow change
everything, seemed as theatrical and obsolete as the medals on
the Beatles' military tunics.

AFTER MY FATHER and mother called it quits, she awoke always at five in the morning and lay in bed, thinking that my
father would come to his senses, walk out on the woman for
whom he had walked out on her, and return home, to his side
of the bed, where he belonged. So far as I know, my father had
no intention of ditching my stepmother or her children, with
whom, with every good intention, he had formed a second
family; and when it turned out that my mother wasn't going
to choose a permanent replacement for Dad's side of the bed, I
began to spend as much time as I could away from my own bed,
too. I used to daydream myself into other families, and some
of them actually took me in and let me live, without pauses, in
the kind of extended living and eating plan that the early 1970s
seemed to specialize in.

If the melody of "She's Leaving Home" now sounds melodramatic almost to the point of parody, I can still read in the words the strangely disembodied feeling my nine-year-old self tried on when I first encountered the song: Was this how it felt to break free from home? To abandon or to be abandoned? The story of my house and the household in the song did not match, but since my mother's day always began at five o'clock, the hour of the new day's start in the song, and the hour at which I, too, would soon take my own exits from Eden, the lament of the refrained farewell—"Bye-bye"—still squeezes my heart.

Will Lee, musician

. . . .

I'VE BEEN MAJORLY informed by the Beatles records throughout my entire life—in my career, in my choice of notes and what to play as a studio musician. No matter what the style of music, it was always a bit of "What would the Beatles have done here?" And that guided me into making good musical choices.

I was probably eleven when the Beatles came to the U.S. I remember how it felt when I first heard their stuff. It was so fresh and so interesting at a time when pop music was just not as adventurous. When they first hit the airwaves with "I Want to Hold Your Hand," you knew something was going on, something different and exciting. Before you even got to see them live there was already this really fresh sound.

The Beatles actually allowed me to have this gig on what's now called *The Late Show with David Letterman*. I've had it since 1982—and that, in my profession, is what you call a steady gig. Plus it takes place [at the former Ed Sullivan Theater] right where the Beatles were first seen in the U.S.!

The first time I was approached to do it, [Letterman's music director] Paul Shaffer said, "You know there's this pilot coming up, it's a TV talk show / music / show comedy / whatever, and it's thirteen weeks." I thought to myself, "Thirteen weeks of solid work?" I'd not had anything like that before. And it just kept getting extended and extended and extended. I feel so lucky.

It was almost too obvious, because of how infatuated I was with the Beatles, for me to even think about having a Beatles band. Traditionally, these have been ones where the musicians pretended to be the Beatles, and even tried to look like them, and that's just not for me—it's hard enough just being yourself, much less being somebody else.

I've enjoyed the great luxury of not being easily pigeonholed by the entire music community in my career. People couldn't put a label on me. I've always loved the fact that jazz guys thought I was a rock guy and rock musicians thought I was a jazz guy. So the idea of me being "Oh, he's the Beatles guy" was always scary to me and I never wanted to go there, but once I'd kind of established myself, I was comfortable enough to come up with this idea after I met our drummer, Rich Pagano.

Rich and I met on a gig together, a small European tour with Hiram Bullock, the late jazz guitarist, who hired us each separately for this tour. By the time we got on stage and started hearing each other it was "Whoa, I wonder what this guy knows about Beatles music."

I heard something in Rich's playing and his singing—he had a very Ringo style of drumming and a very John Lennon style of singing. I started asking him questions and next thing I know our conversations were just Beatles, Beatles, Beatles. We drove poor Hiram crazy. He was like, "Are you guys talking about the Beatles again?"

After the little tour was over I went back to the U.S. and resumed my life. I was in the China Club here in New York City one night listening to someone play. I was standing next to the guy who booked the music at that club and I leaned over and asked, "If I put together a Beatles band, would you hire us to play here?" He said "Yes!" I went home and called Rich Pagano. That was in early 1998.

I REALIZED THAT the magic of the Beatles records, all that great music, couldn't be duplicated with a four-piece band. I knew from the beginning that it had to be at least five pieces; four weren't going to be enough to bring the magic from the records to the stage. Many of the recordings have great percussion parts, great keyboard parts, and massive double vocals.

As a studio singer, I knew that with five people you'd be able to get double vocals, and it would be just beautiful. That kind of gang vocal sound the Beatles had on those records is magical to me—there are a lot of guys singing parts.

I immediately arrived at Jimmy Vivino as the next choice for the band—he's such a musical archivist and so knowledgeable about sounds and music, what the right notes are, things like that. And he also sang. Jack Petruzzelli and Frank Agnello were the final choices—just the greatest couple of guys.

Fab Faux is made up of the same five people as it was back in 1998. In New York City, that's incredible. It may be some kind of record, not counting the Ramones (I don't know how long they lasted). It's amazing. We just do Beatles. And that's all we're here to do. We all have our solo careers but when we five get together it's for one purpose and that's what's so beautiful. When we get on stage there are no arguments. We all agree on exactly what we're doing.

We don't really go for fake British accents. We don't do that kind of thing at all. We just do the music note for note. It's a little bit as if you saw a classical orchestra performing the works of a classical composer.

We take some risks in that obviously some of the Beatles records were two minutes and four seconds long, or something, and you don't really want it to end that fast. Instead of fading out we'll stretch that fade. We ask ourselves what would have happened if this record had kept going? We've done that with "Strawberry Fields," "Day Tripper," "Come Together," "Tax Man," "Paperback Writer," and "Everybody's Got Something to Hide Except Me and My Monkey," and others. These things turn into full-on jams. It's fun because the guys in the band play well enough to actually say something interesting in that extra time. We have something to say beyond copying just those two minutes, so it ends up being satisfying.

Our core audience is now made up of people who already know us. Some people come because they know our names as the semicelebrities that some of us are. The audience members I've enjoyed meeting are the ones who've said things to the effect of "I never really liked the Beatles but I love what you guys are doing." That to me is really interesting.

I'm so guarding of the Beatles that the people I relate to the most are those who, after this many years, have finally come to see their first Fab Faux show and tell me they didn't come before because they didn't want to hear anybody "botch up the Beatles' music." That's just how I would have been. I wouldn't have gone to a Fab Faux show because I don't want anybody messing up their songs.

The generational thing has crossed over from one to another to another to where the parents who were originally Beatles fans bring their kids or even their kids' kids. And those kids become our audience. It's really incredible how it's transcended the generations. The Beatles' appeal goes beyond music. Obviously, they changed fashion, as well; I mean the kind of haircut I wear today would have gotten me beat up in the days before the Beatles came!

When Paul McCartney put on his post 9/11 concert—it was called the Concert for New York City—eleven or twelve years ago, I was asked to play bass with him and his band on the songs on which he played piano or guitar. I was very nervous at the first rehearsal because I was playing with Paul. I came up to him and said "I have a confession to make." I know he has a dislike for Beatles bands—I think he associates them with the ones that are pretending to be the Beatles, that kind of thing. I was trying to let him down gently and tell him that we have this Fab Faux band that honors the later music, the sort of heretofore-thought-of-as-being-impossible-to-perform-live Beatles stuff.

He specifically asked me, "Do you do 'Tomorrow Never Knows?'" and I said, "Oh, absolutely." It turned out that our conversation was filmed; it was featured in a documentary about ten years later called *The Love We Make*. There's me telling Paul about the band exactly as I remembered it.

The great thing is that back when I first heard the Beatles I could have been just a foolish kid who didn't know what he was hearing. But I was right about this band and that's a really good feeling. Especially when you're a little kid making decisions. I'm really glad my investment in them paid off so well, that I still feel the same way. I feel right about my decision, about how much I liked their stuff.

I CAME FROM a musical family—my parents were both pretty good jazz musicians. The Letterman show is just a really great thing that happened to me as a result of having them as parents and then having the Beatles influencing me throughout my career. I got really established as a studio musician, I got thought of as a guy who could just sort of do anything, and that was pretty great.

I'm playing all the time with different people. There's always some stuff going on because New York City is a really great place to be a musician and a for-hire guy. All kinds of things happen here.

Why Couldn't They Leave Us Alone?
by Sigrid Nunez

I REMEMBER WISHING that they were called something else. Even the story about how they came up with their name, originally inspired by Buddy Holly's Crickets (for a while they were the Silver Beetles) made me cringe. It wasn't just the awful pun. The Beatles (like the Crickets) was the kind of name a group of boys would write on the door of their clubhouse. The kind of boys girls my age had lost patience with and were dying to leave behind.

It was even worse when they began to be called the Fab Four. Not that the Beatles themselves were to blame for that. But why couldn't they be called something more dignified? It pained me when it was pointed out how silly their name was. And it was pointed out a lot. A perfect name for them! one of my teachers jeered. School dropouts who can't spell and who look like they crawled out from under a rock.

Looking back, it's hard to believe those four smiling young men with the Cub Scout name who almost always dressed in suits and ties appeared to so many as filthy degenerates.

In the beginning, it seemed one was always defending them.

The first time I ever heard the name was at a pajama party (no one said *sleepover* then). This was when they were already big in the UK but had not yet appeared in the States. Of the five girls at the party, only one of us knew who the Beatles were. The way she described them left me doubtful about the excitement bordering on hysteria that had supposedly taken hold overseas. Not only was there the dumb name. There were the hairdos, described by my friend (pretty accurately, as it turned out) as being like Moe's.

Moe? I hated the Three Stooges. So did every girl I knew. Impossible that anyone bearing even the slightest resemblance to Moe Howard could be another Frank Sinatra or Elvis or Fabian. Whatever had infected those British birds, it could not happen here.

Beatlemania: I remember being asked all the time to explain it and never knowing what to say. Now I would say it was like drinking a potion. All of a sudden you were possessed. You were in love and you wanted something—someone. Someone you'd never met and could never ever have. What to do with these strange, strong feelings? You screamed and jumped up and down for joy but you also cried a lot. Some forgot to eat. Some vomited. Many fainted. A new kind of love, not grown-up love but not just a crush, either, not puppy love. More like being under a spell.

When you tried to explain about the music, people rolled their eyes. How could it be about the music when, given a chance to hear the band live (a chance that I, alas, would never have), fans screamed so loud that the microphones might as well have been off?

Good question (and one that troubled the Beatles as well).

I remember watching one of the many TV broadcasts about the Beatles' first visit to America: a girl not much older than I explaining herself with remarkable poise. I had never heard anyone so young be so articulate. (A teenager invited to express herself in this way, grown-ups actually listening to what she had to say: this in itself was something new. An early sign of what was about to hit with astonishing force: the whole world's attention focussed on youth.)

To the question why fans would want to drown out a band they'd waited in line for hours to get tickets to hear, she responded with serene defiance: What are you talking about? I was there, and I heard every note. I heard every syllable of every song.

Good answer.

But who were these girls, the ones who got to be *there*, shrieking themselves inside out at Carnegie Hall and Shea Stadium? Who were that lucky few hundred who managed to be in the studio for *The Ed Sullivan Show*? Why, oh, why couldn't I have been at least among the thousands to greet them when they landed for the first time, four demigods touching earth at the airport we were all just learning to call Kennedy (the president's assassination had occurred not quite three months before). I was considered too young to be allowed to go into Manhattan without an adult, and I remember that the envy I felt for those girls who got to be *real* fans—seeing the band perform live, mobbing their hotels, chasing their limos, getting autographs—seemed a wicked injustice. Not too many years earlier I'd had a similar feeling about the kids who got to be Mouseketeers. Was life always going to be unfair to me?

To have the full experience, you had to have a favorite. Paul was the most popular; Ringo, the least. This, of course, had everything to do with looks. Always underappreciated, Ringo was the least handsome (and the shortest) of the four. He was odd-looking, in fact, with his hound-dog eyes, froggy mouth, and big, unshapely nose, though it seems to me that precisely because of his unconventional features the moptop suited him better than it did anyone else. I didn't really have a favorite, but when pushed I would declare Ringo. He needed me. It helped also that, of the four, he came from the poorest background, that as a small child he'd been abandoned by his father and had been an unusually sickly boy, spending years in children's hospitals. All this touched a chord in me.

As the old footage shows, all the Beatles were—early on, anyway — incorrigible cutups. John was the drollest, the quickest on his feet. But Ringo was the most natural and appealing clown. And, as much as I disliked the name of the band, I loved the nickname Ringo.

But, as any true fan could tell you, part of the miracle that was the Beatles was that they were *all* great, and that each, in his own way, was adorable and easy to love. In the beginning, you never heard anyone say I don't like this one or that one; only after the band broke up did fans find themselves on Team John or Team Paul.

For me, if anything needed explaining it was Beatlephobia. I remember the phrase *like something that crawled out from under a rock* was heard a lot. So was the word *faggots*. (What other reason could there have been for the long hair, or for the drummer's fondness for wearing several rings at once?) That their music was without a shred of artistic value, that they were a menace to society, sexual perverts with a diabolical ability to create mass hysteria—charges that caused them to be banned from performing in several countries, including Israel and the USSR. What in heaven's name was behind this overwrought response?

You call that music? a friend's father shrieked, spastic with rage. And when do you think was the last time those creeps had a bath?

Talk about hysteria.

To this day I have not forgiven an uncle of mine who happened to be visiting us the night the Beatles first appeared on *Ed Sullivan*, and who by his loud, mean-spirited mockery so thoroughly ruined the experience for me that I wept. Later I learned that parents of young girls everywhere had responded to the Beatles' appearance that night by turning the television off.

And there was Mrs. T., a teacher I'd always particularly liked. One day she brought to school a newspaper article, which she had me stand up and read in front of the class. A fatuous editorial about how the writer and her husband had cured their daughter of Beatlemania by pretending that they, too, had gone ape for the band. I remember the smug tone of the piece and my feeling of outrage at the smirking pleasure the woman appeared to take in having killed her daughter's passion. And I remember how betrayed I felt by Mrs. T.'s stupidity. She had chosen me to read the article precisely because I shared the girl's feelings. A hateful thing to do. Before that day I'd

always done very well in Mrs. T.'s class; after, I no longer cared
to. And when, much concerned, she asked me what it was all
about, I would not speak. Let her figure it out.

But what had gotten into all these parents and teachers?
How could one trust them anymore—about anything? Brain-
washed, delusional, sex-crazed, moronic sheep was how they
described us. Why couldn't they just leave us alone?

On the other hand, my heart went out to those wounded
and frustrated boys—the heartthrobs in pompadours and crew
cuts who all of a sudden found themselves spurned by girls
who used to swoon for them and to whom they now looked all
wrong. (Devastating, the Beach Boys would one day confess,
the discovery that, overnight, you were no longer cool.)

Of course, as the rest of the decade would show, we poor
deluded girls had been on to something all right. It seemed the
more the Beatles played together the more brilliant and magical the music became. They got older, they changed, and we
changed with them. We became hippies together, and the boys
caught up, saying good-bye to crew cuts and pompadours, letting their hair grow, growing beards and sideburns and moustaches, digging the music as devotedly as we female fans.

There's a well-known illustration, drawn sometime in the
mid-sixties by an artist who, inspired by the famous song, tried
to portray what John, Paul, George, and Ringo (they were always named in that order) might look like at sixty-four. It is poignant to think that two of them did not live to see that age—as
it is to recall that once, musing about the toll of superstardom,
John said, "I don't want to die at forty." (The very year . . .)

Once they split up, John was the only Beatle who interested me anymore, though not for much longer.

One night in 1978, at a premiere gala at Lincoln Center, I saw John and Yoko among the guests. He was wearing a tuxedo and the wire-framed glasses whose style had come to bear his name. He was clean-shaven, and his hair, which had begun to recede on top, was thin and dry and so unflatteringly cut that it didn't look like a professional job. As often happens with celebrities encountered in the flesh, he was smaller than I'd always thought he was. He did not look very handsome; with age his face was growing pinched.

No one in the dense crowd was paying any special attention to him; he was just another guest. I don't remember feeling much myself. By that time I'd left the Beatles far behind. I could not have told you what any of them was up to those days, and while the early hits remained—remain—indelible, I did not always recognize their new work when I heard it. Besides, I was now well into my twenties and at a stage in life when . . . well, if you thought I was going to bat an eye just because I happened to be breathing the same air as John Lennon, you were quite wrong. The truth is, there were several people present that night whom I admired much more than I admired him.

Nevertheless, it did amuse me to think what would have ensued had this late fulfillment of my ardent adolescent dream triggered a relapse and I had suddenly burst into maniacal screaming.

Hard to imagine. But oh, how much harder to imagine that, two years hence, a deranged soul believing himself half devil, half Holden Caulfield, would approach John as he left his home on Central Park West, get his autograph, wait for hours for him to return . . .

When I first heard the news of his death, I felt as if someone had murdered my girlhood.

And even then there was someone to scoff. I remember how the man I was living with at the time, himself never a Beatles fan, could not stop criticizing the media for treating the death like a major world event, and me for overreacting.

Some years ago when I was working on a book—a novel in which the main character takes a long hard look back at the sixties, the era when she came of age—I found that a certain Lennon-McCartney song kept coming into my head. A song I've always loved, perhaps my favorite Beatles song, not only their version but the various covers, in particular the one by Judy Collins: "In My Life." And one day it struck me. That gentle meditation on love and loss, that tender look back, that song that might be the perfect anthem of nostalgic middle age, was written when the Beatles were in the full bloom of youth, the year Lennon turned twenty-six and McCartney twenty-four.

If I could have known about the coming day when an assassin would blow away the part of him that was mortal, I think I would have looked harder at John Lennon that night when I was so blasé. I might even have tried to get closer. I would not have been so worried about being uncool. I would have forgotten everyone else but him. I would have stared and stared.

Leah Silidjian, fan

. . . .

MY MOM GOT my dad tickets to see this tribute show, *Rain: A Tribute to the Beatles—On Broadway*, a couple of years ago, in January 2010, when I was fifteen. I wasn't really sure if I wanted to go. I thought, "Oh my god, it's another one of those old bands that nobody likes anymore."

But then I went to the show, and I said to myself, "All right, they were pretty good. It wasn't a *complete* waste."

So then I was listening to the Beatles' music because my dad was playing it a lot and I thought, "You know what, actually, they're pretty good!" And my friends started getting into them and we were listening to them and oh my god, we were raving.

If I hadn't gone to the show I probably wouldn't really like them. But I went to the show and started listening to the music and I really got into them. My friends and I are crazy about them.

I think what I like most about the Beatles is that they were constantly looking for ways to stay ahead, and they weren't afraid to speak their minds and write about what really mattered to them. I mean they each had their own quirks, like John had his wit, and George had his spirituality, and Paul had his charm, and Ringo had his subtle sense of humor.

I THINK IT was last year that we went through this whole phase, this crazy phase, and four of my friends dressed up as the Beatles for Halloween. We made Sgt. Pepper costumes and that was when there was a huge snowstorm over here [in the wake of Hurricane Sandy] and nobody was allowed to go out trick or treating but we went out anyway because we'd made these costumes and we were all excited. My friends and I would spend hours upon hours discussing the Beatles.

We were obsessed. It's not as obsessive now, but the Beatles are still one of my favorite bands.

Probably George is my favorite.

There are a lot of bands in our school, I don't know if you've heard of them, there's Dead End, Rocking One Way, and just a bunch of student-formed bands. Some of them have said, "Oh, you know, the Beatles have influenced us." So I think there are other kids in school who listen to them.

Independence Day, 1976
by Will Hermes

· ·

I TOOK THE E train down to Battery Park with a couple of friends. After unsuccessfully trying to sneak into office high-rises to view the ships, we bought Bud tall boys and wandered the streets with the hordes. We came upon an impromptu TriBeCa street party: some people in a second-floor loft had moved two club-size speaker cabinets into the window, and *Sgt. Pepper's Lonely Hearts Club Band* was thundering out of them. A crowd gathered, dancing and shouting along. People opened their coolers and passed around beers; some precious joints made the rounds. . . .

Happy birthday, America.

For many, pop music still began and ended with the Beatles.

CONTRIBUTORS

· ·

Linda Belfi Bartel is a senior vice president of a management company in Houston.

Roy Blount Jr. is the author of twenty-three books, including *Alphabetter Juice, or The Joy of Text* and *Long Time Leaving: Dispatches From Up South* and a panelist on NPR's *Wait, Wait . . . Don't Tell Me.*

Jamie Nicol Bowles, a painter, art dealer, mother, and wife, is a lifelong Beatles fan. She grew up in Independence, Missouri, and now lives in San Francisco.

Vickie Brenna-Costa lives in Bronxville, New York. She is an artist, lover of music, Francophile, and, more important, David's mother.

Anne Brown works for the National Audubon Society. She spent her earlier years as a general contractor in partnership with her husband; they live in Chapel Hill, North Carolina.

Peter Ames Carlin is the author of *Bruce*, a biography of Bruce Springsteen.

Peter Duchin is a bandleader and pianist.

David Dye is a disc jockey and the host of the nationally syndicated radio show World Café.

Barbara Ehrenreich is a journalist, political activist, and author.

Renée Fleming, the legendary opera singer, is known for the breadth of her repertoire. Her recordings include a rock and roll album, *Dark Hope*.

Joann Marie Pugliese Flood is a photographer in Phoenix, Arizona.

Debbie Geller was a producer for the BBC and the author of *In My Life: The Brian Epstein Story*. She died in 2007.

Henry Grossman's photographs of the Beatles are featured in two recent volumes: *Places I Remember* and *Kaleidoscope Eyes*.

Will Hermes is a journalist and critic.

Janis Ian is a songwriter, singer, musician, and author. She won a Grammy award for the audio version of her memoir, *Society's Child*, in 2012.

Pico Iyer is the author of two novels and eight works of nonfiction, starting with *Video Night in Kathmandu*.

Billy Joel is a musician and composer.

Judy Juanita is a playwright. Her first novel, *Virgin Soul*, was published in 2013.

Gabriel Kahane is a composer and songwriter. His works include the acclaimed *Craigslistlieder* and a musical, *February House*, which was commissioned by New York's Public Theater.

Verlyn Klinkenborg is a member of the New York Times Editorial Board and the author, most recently, of *Several Short Sentences About Writing* and *More Scenes from the Rural Life*.

Cyndi Lauper, the singer and songwriter, won the 2013 Tony Award for Best Original Score for both music and lyrics (for *Kinky Boots*).

Michael Laven ended the sixties by driving his '65 Mustang from the East Coast to California, just missing the Summer of Love. He has had a career in the technology industry based in San Francisco and London.

Fran Lebowitz is a writer and wit.

Will Lee, a jazz and rock musician, is the founder of, and bassist for, the Fab Faux. His latest album is *Love, Gratitude, and Other Distractions*. He has recorded and/or performed live with all four Beatles.

Tom Long is a former roadie and soundman.

Phillip Lopate is a novelist, essayist, and critic. His most recent books are *Portrait Inside My Head* and *To Show and to Tell.*

Greil Marcus is a journalist and music critic who has written extensively about rock 'n' roll.

David Michaelis is the author of biographies of Charles Schulz and N. C. Wyeth. His next one, of Eleanor Roosevelt, will be published in 2015.

"Cousin Brucie" Morrow, a disc jockey for WABC-AM in New York City when the Beatles arrived, is now a host on SiriusXM Satellite Radio.

Mary Norris, a longtime copyeditor at *The New Yorker,* is the author of the forthcoming book *Between You and Me: Confessions of a Comma Queen.*

Sigrid Nunez's most recent book is *Sempre Susan: A Memoir of Susan Sontag.* She is currently working on her seventh novel.

Noelle Oxenhandler's essays have appeared in many national and literary journals. Her latest book is a memoir, *The Wishing Year.*

Joe Queenan is the author of eleven books, including, most recently, *One for the Books*.

Penelope Rowlands, the author of *Paris Was Ours*, *A Dash of Daring*, and other books, is the editor of this collection.

Tom Rush is a singer and songwriter with roots in folk music and the blues. His albums include the folk-inspired *What I Know*.

Anthony Scaduto, Bob Dylan's first biographer, has also written biographies of Mick Jagger, Frank Sinatra, and others.

Carolyn See, author of nine books, is a regular book reviewer for the *Washington Post*. She is working on a memoir.

Lisa See's new novel, *China Dolls*, will be released by Random House in May 2014.

Leah Silidjian is a student at Mahopac High School in Mahopac, New York.

Gay Talese's many books include the memoir *A Writer's Life*. He's now at work on one about his half-century marriage to the well-known book editor Nan Talese.

Laura Tarrish is a designer/illustrator in Portland, Oregon. Her company is Bridgetown Papers.

David Thomson writes about movies. His numerous books include the frequently updated classic *The Biographical Dictionary of Film*.

Vicky Tiel is a fashion designer and the author of the memoir *It's All About the Dress*.

Amanda Vaill is the author of the bestselling *Everybody Was So Young* and other books. Her *Hotel Florida: Truth, Love, and Death in the Spanish Civil War,* is due out from Farrar, Straus & Giroux in April 2014.

Véronique Vienne, a design critic and teacher, is the author of the bestselling *The Art of Doing Nothing*, among other books.

SOURCES AND PERMISSIONS

. . . .

(alphabetical by author)

The letter by Vickie Brenna-Costa, as well as her comment on Facebook, are reprinted with her permission.

The diary excerpt by Anne Brown is reproduced with permission of its author.

The Bruce Springsteen excerpt is from *Bruce* by Peter Ames Carlin. New York: Touchstone, 2012

Barbara Ehrenreich's paragraph is from *Dancing in the Streets: A History of Collective Joy*. New York: Metropolitan Books, 2007.

America's Beatlemania Hangover was originally published online on BBC.UK.com and is reprinted with the kind permission of the Estate of Debbie Geller.

Excerpt from "1976: These are the Days, My Friends" from *Love Goes to Buildings on Fire: Five Years in New York That Changed Music Forever* by Will Hermes. Copyright © 2011 by